Indian Cuisine for the Busy Vegetarian
and anyone pressed for time!

ISBN 9780578651880 (paperback)

First edition published July 2020

www.busyvegetariankitchen.com
 @busyvegetariankitchen

Indian Cuisine

for the

Busy Vegetarian

and anyone pressed for time!

Varu Chilakamarri

For mommy

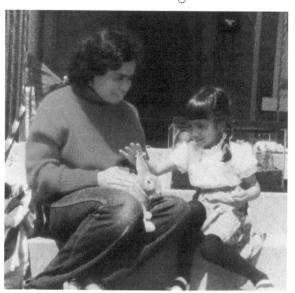

Table of Contents

Recipes

GO-TO GRAINS

DESSERTS IN A DASH

✎ Vegan (These recipes, as written, do not require dairy, eggs, or honey. Note that many of the other recipes can also be made vegan using dairy substitutes.)

Introduction

As a kid, I rarely wanted to eat any of the traditional Indian food that my mom cooked. Her dinners replicated the old-style vegetarian feasts that she and my dad ate in South India: spicy lentil stews with steaming hot rice, cool coconut chutneys, crispy potato wedges, and always lots of ghee. Not wanting to see me starve, my poor mom would often surrender to my complaints and make me fish sticks for dinner—after she had toiled over an elaborate Indian meal for the grownups. But I got my just deserts when I decided to become a full-fledged vegetarian in high school. For a while, I was the kind of vegetarian who subsisted on cheese pizza. By the time I finally realized that Indian food is actually one of the richest cuisines in the world for vegetarians, I was living on my own and far from the unlimited supply that I had in my youth. So, I turned to my mother.

After celebrating her little victory, my mother graciously (and mostly over the phone) walked me through many of the recipes that she had learned from her mother in India. It was amazing what I could remember about the flavors, textures, and ingredients of the food that I had snubbed in the fourth grade. Throughout college and law school, I learned some of the secrets of Indian cooking, one recipe at a time. Before big exams, my friends' moms would send them care packages full of cookies and popcorn balls. Mine would send me a box of lentils and dried chilies. She'd remind me to eat in a note that contained just enough exclamation points to reveal the hidden hysteria of an only child's mother.

While I enjoyed learning the recipes that my mom was teaching me, it was a constant negotiation. The techniques were too time consuming and the recipes always seemed to require some ingredient that I didn't have. Our late-night phone conversations would go something like this:

Me: "I've eaten nothing but fast food all week. I just want some tomato dal."

Mom: "Okay, you'll need two ripe tomatoes—"

Me: "Okay... [reaching into the fridge] Eeew! These tomatoes are moldy . . . it couldn't have been that long since I went to the store. Ugh. It's too late to go tonight."

Mom: "Well, maybe you can make something else."

Me: "Oh! I have pasta sauce, can I use that instead of tomatoes?"

Mom: "What?! No! What are you thinking?! That will taste nothing like tomato dal."

Me: "Hmm … [inspecting the jar]. I think this sauce will work just fine. Why not? It says right here that it's made from tomatoes, well, 'tomato puree,' anyway. Ooh, next time I'll just buy canned tomatoes, they're mold-resistant! Okay, what next?"

Mom: [Audible sigh] "Well, I doubt that will work, but I know you'll do it anyway. You'll also need two green chilies and some urad dal…."

Me: "About that…."

Somehow though, the tomato dal always got made. Through trial and error, I modified many of the recipes and created new ones to fit my lifestyle and whatever I had in the fridge. I took and created shortcuts, while still trying to remain true to the flavors of my childhood. I knew I was onto something when my mom asked me to make her my faux chicken korma when she visited.

If you're anything like me, you're full of good intentions when it comes to cooking and buying fresh ingredients. Maybe you're even familiar with that weekly trip to the grocery store where you've filled your cart with healthy greens, thinking that this week will be different. But your schedule is difficult to predict and it's a lot easier to order pizza than spend a few hours cooking. Before you know it, it's Saturday morning and you open the fridge to find bags of green goopy leaves—a guilty reminder of that trip down the produce aisle long ago.

I'm an attorney in Washington, D.C. Sometimes, after a long day of staring at a computer screen, endless meetings, and conference calls, all I want to do when I get home is pour a glass of wine, dive into a pint of cookie dough ice cream, and call it a night. The last thing many of us have time for is prepping and soaking lentils overnight, grinding spices and nuts into a paste, or stirring hot milk on the stove for hours—steps that many Indian recipes seem to demand.

While fresh ingredients are always preferable and authentic techniques can result in terrific flavor, we are often faced with two different options altogether: spontaneous and quick cooking, or not cooking at all. I've learned that cooking—even for 20 minutes—can be tastier, cheaper, healthier, and sometimes even more efficient than eating out. Indian cooking is not known for its simplicity, but it doesn't have to be that way. Through the inventive use of everyday ingredients and some good old-fashioned secret cooking tips, you can turn this complicated cuisine into something quick, simple, and delicious. This book is your guide to the shortcuts that I adopted after all those late-night conversations with my mom, when I learned to cook Indian food my way.

I recently lost my mom. But amidst the sadness, I feel very grateful for all she gave me. And, thanks to her abundant patience and teachings, I get to remember a part of her whenever I'm in my kitchen. I hope to share that with you here. As my mom would say at the end of every note or email about food . . . Enjoy!!!!

Ingredients: What Do I Really Need?

This book is for those who want to enjoy the wonderful flavor and diversity of Indian food in a time crunch. For that reason, most of the ingredients used here are non-perishable or will at least last in your cupboard or fridge for a while, so that you can whip up a meal on *your* timetable. When a recipe does require fresh ingredients, I've tried to make sure that the recipe accounts for the time it will actually take you to peel, chop, and otherwise prep this stuff. Personally, it drives me crazy when a recipe hides all the real work in the ingredient list with items like "one-third cup of finely chopped onion" or "four boiled eggs." I'm not going to assume that you've got your own little sous chef running around setting up tiny bowls of finely minced herbs in your kitchen! If you've got to do the prep work, the recipe will make that clear.

As for the actual ingredients, I know what you might be thinking. I've often heard the complaint from my best friend: Indian cooking requires too many exotic ingredients. In response, this book tries to simplify some of the more tedious and time-consuming recipes, by leaving out spices and other ingredients that didn't seem strictly necessary. But I've also come to realize that Indian cooking is like baking in this respect. If you've never baked before, the first time can seem like a total pain because you have to stock your cupboard with flour, baking powder, baking soda, vanilla extract, and who knows what else—just to make a batch of cookies! But weeks later, when you want to make your sweetie a birthday cake, you've already got everything you need. Indian food is the same way—just think of it as a little upfront investment. Once you get the basic ingredients, you can make almost anything. So, here's a little guide to a minimal, but well-stocked, Indian pantry.

Spices

Spices are crucial for Indian food, but they are also kind of a mystery. There are so many different kinds—whole seeds, ground powders, dried pods—it's very easy to get overwhelmed. Stick with me and we'll get through this painlessly. At the beginning of the next chapter, I'll give you the quick and dirty tutorial about actually cooking with spices (oil infusion and the like).

For now, let's talk about what you need. In my kitchen I have two categories of spices: whole spices and ground spices.

These are the "whole spices" that I use most often:

o   Black/Brown Mustard Seeds
o   Cumin Seeds
o   Coriander Seeds
o   Crushed Red Pepper Flakes
o   Fenugreek Seeds

You can find most of these spices in the regular grocery store, but some are a bit more obscure. For example, you'll have better luck finding black mustard and fenugreek seeds at an Indian grocery store or online. Yellow mustard seeds are easier to find in regular grocery stores, but they have a spicier, tangier flavor, so they're not a great substitute.

Although not exactly considered a "whole spice," I also keep dried lentils in my spice box, including white lentils (urad dal) and little chickpea lentils (chana dal). These lentils are sometimes roasted together with whole spices to add a little extra crunch. I usually consider them to be optional.

Ground spices are easier to find in supermarkets. These are the ground spices that I use most often:

o   Ground Turmeric
o   Ground Cumin
o   Ground Ginger
o   Ground Red Pepper
o   Curry Powder
o   Garam Masala Powder
o   Ground Cloves
o   Ground Cinnamon
o   Ground Cardamom

Curry powder and garam masala powder are spice blends that save you a lot of time but can be tricky to use at first because they come in many varieties, with varying degrees of intensity and heat. Personally, I'm not picky about the type I use. You'll get familiar with your product of choice and can adjust the amount you use accordingly. Curry powder generally contains some combination of turmeric, cumin, coriander, and red pepper powder. Garam masala is a dark brown spice mixture that has a sweeter, more Christmasy-blend flavor than curry powder. (Okay, so that's probably not how they would describe it in India, but it's got more of the cloves, cardamom, and cinnamon, so you get the picture.) When red pepper powder is called for, you can use red pepper/chile powder (like Kashmiri chile powder) or a lesser amount of ground cayenne pepper. Red pepper powder is sometimes made from a blend of different types of red chilies and may helpfully be labeled "mild" or "hot" in Indian grocery stores. Finally, I also sometimes use asafoetida powder (also called "hing"), which is found in Indian grocery stores. It provides a mild onion-like flavor, and I usually list it as optional.

Rice and Grains

There are many varieties of rice, from short to long grain, white to brown, jasmine to basmati. Unless otherwise specified in a recipe, use whatever kind you like! Generally, basmati is slightly more expensive than your basic white rice, but it has a nice aroma and does not mush together as much, so it's a good bet for most recipes, and your rice will look like it came from a restaurant. But your basic long grain rice will work for almost anything too. Brown rice has a bit more bite than white rice and generally takes a little longer to cook, so it wouldn't be my top choice for most of the rice dishes in this book, although that's just a personal preference. You could certainly eat any of the lentil and curry dishes alongside plain brown rice. I also always have farina cereal/cream of wheat (non-instant) on hand for making savory and sweet Indian porridges and crepes.

Lentils

Lentils are a major source of protein for vegetarians, and there are a lot of vegetarians in India. As a result, a ton of different lentils are used in Indian cooking—red, white, black, brown, yellow, oily, and split lentils are very common. Red lentils are the fastest lentils to cook and they have now found their place in

regular grocery stores across the United States. To keep things easy, all my lentil recipes can be made with red lentils (but you can certainly experiment with other varieties). Red lentils are often called "split red lentils," or "masoor dal." Uncooked, they look like tiny bright orange discs. Red lentils are milder than brown lentils—the most technical way of putting it is that they taste less "lentily." Also, unlike brown lentils, which you might have had in minestrone soup, red lentils do not retain their disc-like shape when cooked. So cooked red lentils have more of a mashed potato-like consistency and are easier to digest. You can cook lentils almost the same way you cook rice, but with a bit more water. Unlike rice, red lentils release a lot of foam as they cook, so always be sure to use a big enough pot so they don't overflow!

Preserved Veggies and Fruits

Fresh vegetables are great, and you should use them whenever possible. But for busy people who want to make a good Indian meal after an exhausting day of work, fresh vegetables may not always be realistic. So, our default in this book is to use canned or frozen vegetables wherever they work. Usually, that cuts out a lot of that hidden prep time in a recipe and you can keep these goods on hand for weeks or months, so you can make a meal even if you weren't able to stop at the market this week. Keep in mind that you can add fresh veggies in place of canned or frozen ingredients whenever you want—you'll just need to adjust the cooking time.

These are the preserved foods that I use most often:

- o   Canned diced or crushed tomatoes
- o   Canned diced or whole potatoes
- o   Canned tomato sauce
- o   Canned chickpeas
- o   Ginger paste (in a tube)
- o   Bottled minced garlic
- o   Bottled lemon juice
- o   Canned tamarind juice
- o   Tamarind concentrate paste
- o   Frozen peas
- o   Raisins

Nut Butters

We've come a long way since the plain old peanut butter and jelly sandwich. Now, you can get all kinds of nut butters. I always have ground cashew or almond butter on hand for curries. You can find these nut butters in many grocery stores and natural food stores, right next to the peanut butter. Be warned, these nut butters can give you sticker shock—they cost more than double your kid's peanut butter. But take comfort in the fact that just a few spoons will go a long way to creating a meal that will rival your favorite takeout korma.

Meat Substitutes

When I became a vegetarian, I was eternally grateful for the many faux vegetarian meat options that exist. While Indian food is known around the world for having a wide range of vegetarian options, some of the meatier North Indian dishes are the most popular in Indian restaurants in the United States. I didn't want us vegetarians to feel left out, so I came up with some modified faux meat versions, for those of you who like the taste and texture of meat substitutes. I've found chicken substitutes like Morningstar Farms' Meal Starters Chik'n Strips, Quorn's Naked Chik'n Cutlets, and Beyond Meat work particularly well, but any number of brands could work. These faux meat options are available in the freezer aisle of most grocery stores.

Yogurt and Cheese

Plain yogurt is widely used in Indian cooking. When a recipe in this book calls for yogurt, you can use any brand of plain yogurt. I prefer regular yogurt to Greek yogurt, but you can use either—just note that because Greek yogurt is thicker, you might want to thin it a bit with a few spoons of water for some recipes.

Fresh cheese called "paneer" is also used in many Indian recipes. Making homemade paneer is a fun project, but it takes some time and planning. You can also find paneer in some natural food stores and ethnic markets. Firm tofu works well as a substitute in favorite dishes like palak paneer and matar paneer, so tofu is often the default for my recipes. While tofu does not taste like paneer, its texture is similar and it's ready to cook straight out of the box. (You can also sometimes substitute other fresh soft cheeses like fresh mozzarella.)

Where the heck do I find this stuff?

These days, everyone's a foodie. That means you have to put up with more terms like "balsamic reduction" and "panko" creeping into our lexicon. And you've got people like me thinking they can write cookbooks! But the good news is that it's also a lot easier to find exotic ingredients. And when you can't find it locally, you can always turn to the internet. It wasn't always this way. Growing up in Ohio, I watched my parents struggle to find the essential ingredients for Indian home-cooking. Back then, there was no "Indian" grocery store nearby and we didn't have a car, so we'd take the bus to a Chinese supermarket across town. We'd walk right past fish heads and mung beans until we got to the shelf dedicated to South Asian foods. There, among the packets of lentils with funny lettering and boxes of spices that looked exhausted from their intercontinental travels, my mom was in her comfort zone.

Most of the ingredients used in this book are widely available in regular grocery stores. Often, you'll find better deals on spices, oil, and rice in the Hispanic/International food aisle of the same grocery store. A few spices may be more difficult to find. Items like black mustard seeds, tamarind paste, and yellow and white lentils are often not available in your basic supermarket but are generally available in natural/health food stores or specialty ethnic grocery stores (Indian, Chinese, and Middle Eastern food shops will usually carry these ingredients). If you're going to try a few recipes, I recommend trying to find an Indian grocer in your area. You'll find absolutely everything you need there and can also pick up a few other things to go with your meal, like spicy mango relish, paneer cheese, and Indian candy and desserts. If Indian food is going to be a part of your regular cooking repertoire and you don't live near a specialty grocery store, then I highly recommend online shopping. There are many websites that sell Indian groceries and spices, and some are better priced than many natural food stores. (My go-to source of the moment is: www.ishopindian.com.)

Time-saving supplies

I sometimes work late into the morning hours, with the white noise of the TV as my companion. So naturally, I've come pretty close to buying a variety of special kitchen tools that the infomercials promised would change my life. Who wouldn't want to pulverize a brick and make guacamole with a single machine? Alas, special gadgets never seem to make it out of their probation period in my kitchen. Somehow, they always seem to take up more time and space than I have. So, for the most part, the recipes in this book will not require you to have any unique tools beyond your basic cooking equipment, *i.e.*, pots and pans, good knives, and a cutting board. There are, however, a few items that I use all the time that you may also want to have on hand as you set out on your Indian cooking adventures:

Blender or handheld immersion blender

This one is critical for many recipes. Yes, a regular blender is a bit bulky for tiny kitchens, but trust me, it's well worth the space, not only for making chutneys and some of the other recipes in this book, but for other dishes like soups, smoothies, and of course, margaritas!

I've also found that if you have a blender, you don't really need other choppers. Between you and me, I've even used my blender for grinding coffee beans and whipping cream when my hand-held mixer unexpectedly failed. The best part is that the blender is virtually self-cleaning: after you're done, just add water and a few drops of soap and give it a quick blend to clean! I've also added a handheld immersion blender to my kitchen toolkit—this gadget makes it super easy to blend and partially blend curry sauces directly in the pot.

Potato smasher

There seems to be no replacement for your basic potato smasher. It gets the job done faster than a fork and can be used for much more than mashing potatoes. I use it whenever I want to smooth out the texture of cooked food just a little but don't want it completely pureed. A few whooshes of the potato smasher is all you'll need to finish up the filling for samosas, or to convincingly smash canned tomatoes so that they lose that uniform canned texture.

Metal tongs or metal strainer

If you are going to be making any of the deep-fried snacks in this book (samosas, veggie fritters, gulabjamuns, etc.), I would suggest getting metal tongs or a small metal strainer. You can always get away with using a fork or a slotted spoon to get your delicacies out of the hot splattering oil—my mom did that, but she was tough, and she occasionally burned her hands! I prefer the long metal tongs—they allow you to quickly grab the fried fritter and give it a shake, all while you and your nice blouse remain several feet away from a dry cleaner's nightmare.

Ceramic pot

Years ago, I got tired of continuously opening kitchen drawers with my spice and sauce covered hands, so I used a big red ceramic flowerpot to hold my large knife, wooden mixing spoons, spatulas, and vegetable peeler. It was cute, convenient, and saved me the trouble of rifling through my drawers while something burned on the stove and having to later clean up goopy fingerprints that had not been left by a child. Nowadays you can buy nice utensil holders made for this very purpose.

Kitchen shears

For no other reason except that they matched my red flowerpot, I threw in a pair of red scissors. To my surprise, those scissors became my most useful kitchen tool—be it for quickly opening packages, cutting stubborn stems, or mincing wet cilantro leaves. I've since upgraded to kitchen shears, but any scissors will do!

Quick cooking tips

Besides keeping the cooking equipment fairly simple, there are a few other time-saving techniques which I use every day and that I've tried to weave into the recipes in this book. Many of these are just smart cooking, common sense tips that could be used in any style of cuisine.

Make an agenda

Cooking even a simple Indian meal can involve several dishes. A few moments of planning at the outset can save you a lot of time. First, figure out what you want to make. You can make any combination of dishes that appeals to you, but most of the curry and lentil dishes in this book are best served with some type of rice or naan. Because plain rice is a relatively low maintenance dish, start cooking the rice as soon as you step into the kitchen. Rice generally takes about 15 minutes to cook and should sit for another 5 minutes to cool. In those precious 20 minutes, you can make another item. The same rule applies for most lentil dishes: start cooking the lentils right when you begin. After the rice and lentils are on their way, you can focus on the remaining steps of the meal. A simple meal for me involves plain rice and either lentils or curry, with a side of chutney, raita, or plain yogurt. Another variation would be plain lentils, a rice dish, with a side of steamed vegetables. If I have a bit more time or am cooking for friends, I might make rice, lentils, a curry, and an appetizer.

Set the mood

Sometimes it's hard to escape that nagging feeling that you should be doing something other than cooking. There's always that project you need to finish, those work emails that came in right after you left the office, and a to-do list to conquer. And if you feel this way for too long, well, you might quit cooking before you really get started.

We might not be able to stop this feeling altogether, but why not at least mitigate? If you're only happy multitasking, then multitask! Working, emailing, or texting too much while cooking is usually not advised, but why not multitask in a way that makes things fun? Listen to your favorite podcast or catch up on the news while you cook. Whatever you choose, set the mood in the beginning so that you don't feel like you're "stuck" in the kitchen.

Another way you can bask in the feeling of productivity is by doubling your recipes—make your work count by making extra. The great thing about Indian food is that it's usually even better the next day, after the flavors have had a chance to mingle in the fridge. Leftovers make the perfect lunch that will save you time and money later!

Multi-task

Speaking of productivity, one of the best ways to minimize your kitchen time is ordered multitasking within each recipe. You'll notice that most of the recipes here are broken down in steps, but you are often directed to manage multiple steps at once. For example, while your oil is starting to heat up, the recipe might direct you to chop an onion (which you can do pretty quickly, once you get the hang of it . . . more on that below). Or, while your onions are sautéing, I'll tell you to assemble a curry sauce. I will keep you on your toes! But this is all totally doable . . . just read over the recipe first and have your ingredients handy before you start. If you know what the plan is and proceed through each step efficiently, you will get the most out of your time in the kitchen.

Befriend your microwave

The microwave is underutilized in most cookbooks. But in my view, unless you're heating up a TV dinner, microwaving is a part of cooking and it can save you some critical evening minutes. You don't have to use the microwave if you prefer stovetop cooking or using a rice cooker or pressure cooker. But as a default, my recipes suggest using the microwave whenever it can save you some time.

Cook from your cabinet

I used to have a weekly ritual of throwing out spoiled vegetables found at the bottom of my fridge. I hated the waste and the unpredictability. I often didn't realize that a key perishable ingredient had gone bad until I started cooking, which meant I'd have to go to the grocery store right then or give up! So, I decided to take help where I could get it. I regularly use canned and frozen vegetables and anything else that isn't likely to go bad for a few weeks. That doesn't mean that I don't use fresh vegetables when I can, but I always try to keep enough non-perishables on hand for a few meals.

Learn to chop an onion

Okay, this one's pretty specific, but if there's just one cooking skill that will yield you significant gains in the kitchen, it would be this. Onions are a common ingredient in Indian cooking, so it will save you a lot of time to get this right. I first learned about the "right way" of chopping an onion in Julia Child's classic, *Mastering the Art of French Cooking*, which contains old-school drawings depicting the special horizontal and vertical slicing technique. Now, you can just watch a 2-minute video on YouTube. My recipes generally do not require a finely chopped onion, so you don't have to do this perfectly, but try to follow the general chef's technique for dicing onions and you won't be sorry.

Rescue your food

One of the most intimidating things about cooking Indian food is all the spices and flavors. But remember, cooking is largely an art, not a science. Even after you've dutifully followed all the steps in a recipe, it's usually not too late to rescue your food if something went awry in the flavor department. Flavor is relatively subjective. Some like it hot, some hate cilantro (I can't imagine it, but my heart goes out to you!), and some hate rose water (sorry, that's me!). And that's why cooking is so special—you end up with something tailor-made. I offer specific (medium) spice measurements in these recipes, but don't be afraid to adjust the quantities. Here are some quick tips for doing so:

Too bland? When your food turns out just blasé, mentally run through these four pillars of flavor to make sure each is properly represented: salt, sour, sweet, and hot.

1. Try adding a little extra **salt**, it tends to boost all the flavors of a dish. Add a quarter to half a teaspoon and stir well.
2. If your dish just gets saltier but still seems lackluster, give your food a little dose of **acidity**—add a tablespoon of lemon juice or vinegar and see where that gets you. Repeat as needed.
3. Indian food does not need a lot of **sugar**, but there are times it can help round out the flavors. Try adding a quarter to half a teaspoon.
4. Finally, sometimes you just want to **intensify** the flavor of your dish. When salt and lemon juice just don't cut it, try this:

Heat up half a tablespoon of oil in a small saucepan and then add in a bit of powdered spices. Start with a quarter teaspoon or more of red pepper powder along with half a teaspoon of curry powder. (If there are other powdered spices that were called for in the recipe, add a bit more of those instead.) Stir and melt the spices into your hot oil until you have a nice spice paste. This shouldn't take more than a minute or so. Then, stir this spicy paste into your dish and reheat the whole dish to allow the flavors to cook together.

Repeat this 4-step process until you're happy with your flavors.

Too strong? Now here's the rub. It's trickier to fix something if you've made it too salty or spicy. The only thing that works then is to dilute the flavors. If you're making lentils or a curry, sometimes you can literally dilute the flavors by adding a quarter cup of water. But often, that will just make your dish runnier and no less spicy. If you're making a saucy curry or lentil dish, you can try adding a quarter cup of plain yogurt or a few spoons of sour cream or heavy cream. If you're making a rice dish, you can stir in more plain rice, to dilute intense flavors. This all sounds like a pain, right? It is. The moral of this story is to be a bit conservative with your flavor additions and add salt and spice in small increments so that you avoid an overdose.

Spice note: If you like your food very mild, start out by using only half the red pepper powder or crushed pepper flakes that is called for in the recipes. You can always add in more later!

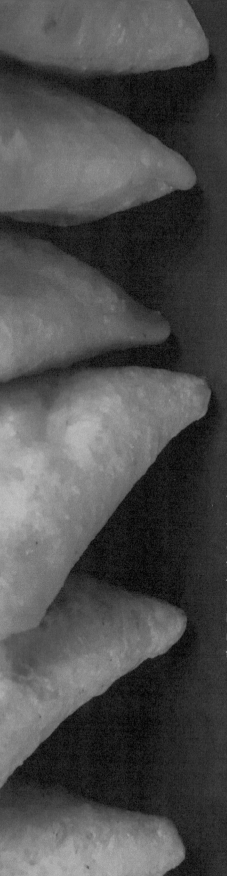

SIMPLE STARTERS & DIPS

Crispy samosas, smoky tandoori skewers, crunchy chaat, and chunky mango chutney are just some of the distinct and mouthwatering snacks that you'll only find in Indian cuisine. In this chapter, we'll make eight quick chutneys and dips, five savory snacks, and two special salads. You can basically mix and match the chutneys with any of the snacks or serve them as dips with crackers, pita, or bread. Either way, these starters are a great introduction to the flavors of Indian food.

As for the execution: there is an easy way and a hard way to make these signature delicacies. You may never have guessed that flour tortillas could make a deliciously flaky samosa shell, or that you could create a restaurant-quality tamarind dip out of nothing but a can of juice, but shortcuts like these will make you the MacGyver of your kitchen and leave even the most reluctant of cooks looking for an excuse to have company over.

Tomato Chutney

Mango Chutney

Coconut Chutney

Cilantro Chutney

Garden-Fresh Raita

Onion-Spiced Raita

Lemon Cilantro Dip

Tamarind Dipping Sauce

Veggie Fritters

Spinach Pakoras

Potato Samosas

"Beef" Samosas

Tandoori Skewers

Palak Paneer Salad

Chaat Salad

Indian Spices: Oil Infusion Demystified

You may have noticed that there are a lot of whole spices used in Indian cooking. Mustard, cumin, and coriander seeds are just a few of the spices that appear in many recipes, particularly in South Indian food. The process of toasting spices in hot oil and then using that infused oil to flavor the food is called "tempering." The toasted spices and oil are called "tadka" or "popu" in some parts of India. For my parents, Indian food was not really Indian food if it didn't start with a little popu. This oil infusion technique is pervasive—it's used when making rice, lentils, and many chutneys.

So how does one go about properly infusing oil? I'm going to be straight with you. In super traditional South Indian cooking, hard spices are not—as I sometimes suggest in this book—simply plopped into hot oil and fried up. Instead, the different spices are put into the hot oil or ghee (clarified butter) in a particular order, so that each spice is cooked just the perfect amount of time for its size. For example, the larger, harder spices such as black peppercorns and cloves might be put into the hot oil first, followed by whole dried chilies, then mustard seeds, and then cumin seeds. Different households have their own method of doing it, but the point is to ensure that harder spices have a little longer to cook and infuse in the oil, while the more delicate ones do not burn.

This all makes perfect sense, but I started out cooking a different way. See, when I was away at college, my mom would sometimes send me special spice mixes in the mail. She knew I wouldn't go spice hunting myself, so she'd send me some essentials. Rather than keeping all the spices separate, she'd just throw them into a plastic bag—after all, I was lucky to be getting anything!

Naturally, I'd just spoon in a mixture of coriander, mustard, cumin, urad dal and chilies into my hot oil at the beginning of every recipe. Now that I understand the process a bit better, I wouldn't recommend commingling all your spices, as different recipes call for different spices and amounts. But remember, we're just making dinner here, so no need to get all stressed out.

I've adopted a simplified, three-step process that you'll see repeated in many of my recipes. In a nutshell: (1) heat the oil; (2) throw in large spices; (3) end by adding in delicate spices and powders. But here's the step-by-step:

Step 1 – Start by heating your oil for about 30 seconds to 1 minute over medium heat. Vegetable oil work best for this, but I'm not going to be one of those sticklers that starts lecturing you on smoke points. (Mostly because I can't really tell the difference given how quickly popu is made, but also because I nearly failed organic chemistry.) Go ahead, use the light olive oil, I won't tell.

Step 2 – Once the oil is hot, add the biggest, hardest spices in your recipe first. Usually this includes peppercorns, coriander seeds, fenugreek seeds, and any lentils that you are roasting, such as chana dal or urad dal. You could also throw in mustard and cumin seeds at this stage, though I tend to wait about 30 seconds or so to add them. You'll want to roast these spices together for about a minute or so. A good indication that these harder spices are sufficiently toasted is when the black mustard seeds lighten in color and begin popping or sputtering. Be careful, these little suckers tend to pop right up at you as you're leaning in to marvel at your awesome cooking.

Step 3 – Add your lighter spices and powders. Usually, this will include ingredients like red pepper flakes, minced garlic and ginger, and any ground spices that you'd like to roast. These will cook very fast—30 seconds to a minute—so be prepared to remove the spices from the heat or to add in the rest of your ingredients at this point.

The lesson here: use common sense, and so long as you don't let anything literally blacken, you'll be fine and your popu will be too!

Tomato Chutney *in 15 minutes*

This is one of the simplest chutneys that you can make straight out of your cupboard in minutes flat. The only problem is that it disappears in even less time!

Ingredients

1	tablespoon of oil
$1/2$	teaspoon of coriander seeds
$1/2$	teaspoon of black mustard seeds
6-8	fenugreek seeds (optional, adds stronger flavor)
$1/4$	teaspoon of crushed red pepper flakes
1	14.5-ounce can of diced tomatoes
$1/4$	teaspoon of turmeric powder
$1/4$	teaspoon of salt

Steps

1 Add the oil to a medium pot over medium heat. After 1 minute, add the coriander and mustard seeds (and fenugreek, if using). Once one or two of the mustard seeds starts popping, add the remaining ingredients. Partially cover and cook on medium heat for 8 minutes, stirring occasionally.

2 Remove from heat and then blend the tomato mixture for 15-20 seconds. (An immersion blender or regular blender works fine. If you are using a regular blender, take care to vent out the steam while blending, as you would when blending a hot soup.)

Serves 2-4.

This flavorful chutney is a great condiment to top or stir into any milder dish, such as yellow potato curry. It also pairs well with coconut chutney and dosas. And in a pinch, just top plain rice and lentils with a dollop of tomato chutney, and you've got a quick and tasty meal!

From the left: Coconut Chutney, Mango Chutney, and Tomato Chutney.

Chutneys are intensely flavored sauces and pastes that are eaten in small quantities and are often used to brighten the main meal. Coconut, mango, and tomato are just a few of the versatile chutneys you can make in minutes.

Mango Chutney *in 20 minutes*

This is a very adaptable recipe. You can use frozen or fresh mango. And, if you have leftover sauce packets from Chinese takeout, then you already have the secret ingredient—sweet and sour sauce. No excuses!

Ingredients

$1^1/_2$ cups of frozen mango chunks (or 1 large mango)
1   tablespoon of oil
4-8 black peppercorns (optional)
1   teaspoon of black mustard seeds
1   teaspoon of cumin seeds
$^1/_2$ teaspoon of crushed red pepper flakes
1   tablespoon of minced garlic (bottled or fresh)
$^1/_4$ teaspoon of ginger powder or paste
$^1/_2$ teaspoon of salt
$^1/_2$ teaspoon of paprika
3   tablespoons of sweet and sour sauce

Steps

1 If you're using frozen mango, move to step 2. Otherwise, peel and cut your fresh mango into bite-size chunks.

2 Add the oil to a medium pot over medium heat. After 1 minute, add the peppercorns (if using), mustard seeds, and cumin seeds. Once one or two mustard seeds start popping, toss in the red pepper flakes, garlic, and ginger. As the garlic turns golden, add your mango, the remaining ingredients, and $^1/_3$ cup of water. Stir thoroughly and partially cover.

3 Simmer over medium heat for about 10 minutes (add 5-10 extra minutes if you're using fresh mango). If the chutney starts to dry out, add a bit more water, a tablespoon at a time. The finished product should have a chunky, jam-like texture.

Serves 2-4.

Serve alongside warm store-bought naan, pita chips, or salty crackers.

Tip: Don't have sweet and sour sauce? Just substitute in 1 tbs of ketchup + 1 tbs of brown sugar + 1 tbs of cornstarch instead!

Coconut Chutney *in 15 minutes*

This unique chutney is a great addition to any spicy meal because of the cooling effect of the yogurt. It's simple to make and is a great side dish to serve with any meal. I use it as a sauce over rice and lentils, and it's often the most memorable item on the table.

Ingredients

1   tablespoon of oil
$1/2$ teaspoon of black mustard seeds
$1/4$ teaspoon of cumin seeds
$1/2$ teaspoon crushed red pepper flakes
1   cup of dried, shredded coconut (unsweetened)
1   cup of plain yogurt
$1/2$ teaspoon of salt

Steps

1   Add the oil to a small pan over medium heat. After 1 minute, add the mustard and cumin seeds. Once one or two mustard seeds start popping, add the red pepper flakes and coconut. Lightly toast the coconut for about 45 seconds and then remove the pan from the heat.

2   Add the ingredients from your pan, along with the yogurt and salt, to your blender. Blend for about 1 minute, or until the ingredients are thoroughly mixed. (You may need to occasionally stop blending and stir the chutney to make sure all of the coconut is blended.) The coconut chutney will be pourable but thick with a nice crunch. It will thicken further after refrigeration.

Serves 2-4.

The chutney should be refrigerated if not immediately served. It can be served cold or at room temperature. Add it to rice or lentils or serve alongside your favorite curry or dosas.

Cilantro Chutney *in 15 minutes*

Ingredients

1   tablespoon of oil
5-8   black peppercorns
$1/2$ teaspoon of black mustard seeds
$1/2$ teaspoon of cumin seeds
$1/2$ teaspoon of crushed red pepper flakes
1   cup of tomato sauce or diced tomatoes
$1/8$ teaspoon of turmeric powder (a pinch)
$1/2$ teaspoon of salt
1   bunch of fresh cilantro (fresh is essential here)

Steps

1   Add the oil to a medium pot over medium heat. After 1 minute, add the peppercorns, mustard seeds, and cumin seeds. Once one or two mustard seeds start popping, add the red pepper flakes, tomato sauce, turmeric, and salt. Stir, cover, and cook. Let the sauce bubble for about 2 minutes and then remove from heat.

2   Roughly chop the entire bunch of cilantro, stems and all. Add the tomato mixture, cilantro, and about $1/4$ cup of water to your blender. Blend for about 1 minute, or until the cilantro is finely minced. (You may need to occasionally stop and stir the chutney to make sure all of the leaves are blended.) The finished chutney should resemble a dark salsa verde.

Serves 2-4.

If you like cilantro, this flavorful chutney is a great accompaniment to any rice or lentil dish. Also try it with tortilla chips or pita.

> **Tip:** Don't have tomato sauce? You can swap in plain marinara! The spices here will generally overpower the marinara, so it's a good substitute.

Garden-Fresh Raita *in 10 minutes*

A lot of people never give plain yogurt a second glance at the grocery store. But plain yogurt is not only healthier than its fruity counterparts, it provides a cool and refreshing balance to any spicy meal. That's why yogurt is a staple in many Indian households and why my mom made a big pot of homemade yogurt every day. I use store-bought yogurt to make these quick side dishes, which I view as a must-have alongside hot curry or lentils.

Ingredients

1	small tomato
$1/2$	a cucumber
1	small handful of fresh mint (optional)
1	cup of plain yogurt
$1/4$	teaspoon of salt
$1/8$	teaspoon of black pepper (a pinch)

Steps

1 Dice the tomato. Chop or shred the cucumber (peel if desired). If you are using fresh mint, chop or tear a handful.

2 Mix all the ingredients, except the mint. You can either refrigerate or serve immediately. If desired, stir in the mint just before serving.

Serves 2-4.

Serve alongside any spicy meal or as a dip for any fried snack or dosas.

From the left: Garden-Fresh Raita and Onion-Spiced Raita.

Onion-Spiced Raita *in 10 minutes*

This raita has the subtle flavors of French onion dip, except it's a totally guilt-free version!

Ingredients

1	onion
1	tablespoon of oil
$1/2$	teaspoon of black mustard seeds
$1/2$	teaspoon of cumin seeds
$1/4$	teaspoon of crushed red pepper flakes
1	cup of plain yogurt
$1/4$	teaspoon of salt
1	handful of fresh cilantro (optional)

Steps

1   Mince half the onion and set aside. You'll want about $1/3$ cup.

2   Add the oil to a small pan over medium heat. After 1 minute, add the mustard seeds and cumin seeds. Once one or two of the mustard seeds start popping, toss in the red pepper flakes and cook for another 30 seconds, before removing from heat.

3   Mix the raw onion, yogurt, and salt with the toasted spices and infused oil. If desired, roughly chop or tear the cilantro and add it to the raita before serving.

Serves 2-4.

Serve alongside any spicy meal or rice, or with chips.

Two Quick Dips

Tamarind dipping sauce and lemon cilantro dip are set apart from the other chutneys in this chapter because they are so simple to make. These quick recipes require no roasting of spices, and they'll keep fresh in the fridge for days. These pair well with any of the savory snacks in this chapter.

I discovered how to make the tamarind dipping sauce during my attempts to replicate that tangy sauce that the restaurants always seem to serve with samosas. I initially tried making it with tamarind paste, but this version uses tamarind juice or nectar and it is perfect. Plus, you can't beat a one-ingredient recipe! You can find the tamarind juice at most supermarkets (check the international or Hispanic food aisles). And the tangy lemon cilantro dip requires no cooking at all. Just pop everything into your blender and you're done!

Lemon Cilantro Dip *in 5 minutes*

Ingredients

1   bunch of cilantro (fresh is essential here)
1   lemon
2   tablespoons of cashew or almond butter
1   teaspoon of minced garlic (bottled or fresh)
$1/2$ teaspoon of salt
$1/2$ teaspoon of olive oil
$1/8$ teaspoon of red pepper powder (a pinch)
$1/8$ teaspoon of sugar (a pinch)

Steps

1   Roughly chop the entire bunch of cilantro, stems and all. Peel and halve the lemon, removing the seeds.

2   Pour $1/4$ cup of water into the blender and add in all the ingredients, including the cilantro and lemon. Pulse for 1-2 minutes or until the cilantro is finely minced. (You may need to occasionally stop and stir the dip to make sure all of the leaves are blended.) The dip should resemble a creamy salsa verde.

Tamarind Dipping Sauce *in 15 minutes*

Ingredients

1   can of tamarind nectar/juice (approximately 10 ounces is enough)

Steps

Pour all the tamarind nectar into a small saucepan and bring it to a boil. Boil, uncovered. A heavy, bubbly foam should form, and after 10-15 minutes of cooking, the tamarind nectar should have reduced to a quarter of its original volume. Turn off the heat and allow the tamarind sauce to cool. Once slightly cooled, you'll be able to determine if the tamarind nectar has reached the desired consistency. (I like it to have the consistency of pancake syrup.) If the tamarind is too thin, boil for another 5 minutes.

Veggie Fritters *in 30 minutes*

Ingredients

6-8 cups of vegetable oil (or enough for deep frying)
1 cup of garbanzo bean/chickpea flour (found in natural food stores)
1 teaspoon of salt
$1/4$ teaspoon of red pepper powder
4 cups of vegetables (any of the following work well: onions, potatoes, yams, squash, tomatoes, broccolini, or frozen broccoli or cauliflower)

Steps

1 If you happen to have a deep fryer, use it! Otherwise, in a large pot, add about 6 cups of oil for frying. The exact amount of oil will depend on the size of your pot, but you basically want enough oil so that your veggie fritters will be fully immersed, but the pot should be no more than half full. Begin to heat the oil over high heat on the back burner. While the oil heats up, move on to steps 2 and 3. (You want the oil to stay right around 350°F in the meantime.)

2 In a large bowl, stir the flour, salt, and red pepper together with $3/4$ cup of water. This will be your batter.

3 Cut the veggies into large chunks. Harder veggies such as fresh potatoes should be cut thinner so that they can cook faster; tomatoes should always be cut or slit. (To prep any frozen veggies, defrost them in the microwave and pat dry.)

4 After the oil has been heating for about 5 minutes, carefully drop in a little batter to test the temperature (it should be at 350°F). If the batter quickly rises to the surface and begins to sizzle, then the oil is ready. (If it browns instantly, reduce the heat a bit and try again in 2 minutes.) Using long metal tongs, dip and coat a few chunks of veggies in the batter and then carefully place them in the hot oil. Repeat until there are about 10 fritters frying in the oil—each fritter should have enough space in the oil so that it can rise to the surface. Turn each fritter so that all sides are golden brown (about 4-8 minutes depending on the veggie). Remove the fritters from the oil and drain on a paper towel. Fry another batch as needed.

Serves 2-4.

Serve immediately with a chutney or ketchup.

Spinach Pakoras *in 20 minutes*

Ingredients

4	cups of vegetable oil (or enough for deep frying)
10	ounces of frozen chopped spinach
2	teaspoons of salt
$^3/_4$	cups of garbanzo bean/chickpea flour
$^1/_4$	cup white rice flour
$^1/_2$	teaspoon red pepper powder
$^1/_4$	teaspoon curry powder
1	tablespoon of lemon juice or vinegar

Steps

1   In a large pot, add about 4 cups of oil for deep frying. (You can also use a deep fryer here, if you have one.) The exact amount of oil will depend on the size of your pot, but you basically want enough oil so that your pakoras will be fully immersed while frying, but the pot should be no more than half full. Begin to heat the oil over medium-high heat on a back burner. Meanwhile, move to step 2. (You want the oil to stay right around 350°F.)

2   Thaw your spinach by microwaving it in a bowl for 2 minutes. Without draining it, combine the spinach with 1 teaspoon of salt (save the remaining salt for later) and the rest of the ingredients. Stir this pakora batter with a fork until thoroughly combined.

3   After the oil has heated for about 5 minutes, carefully drop in a little pakora batter. If the batter begins to sizzle, then the oil is ready. (If it browns instantly, reduce the heat a bit and try again in 2 minutes. You want to keep it at 350°F.) Carefully drop heaping teaspoons of the pakora batter into the hot oil. Repeat this process until the pot is full of pakora balls, or you are out of batter. The pakoras should cook for about 4-6 minutes or until lightly browned and crispy. Remove the pakoras from the oil using metal tongs or a fork and drain on a paper towel. Sprinkle with the remaining salt, as desired.

Serves 4.

Serve hot with tamarind dipping sauce, ketchup, or barbeque sauce.

Tip: To re-use your deep-frying oil for frying similar foods, just pour the cooled oil back into its bottle through a funnel lined with a coffee filter.

Pictured with tamarind dipping sauce.

Potato Samosas *in 50 minutes and totally worth it*

Samosas are ubiquitous in India—from fancy weddings to airport terminals. Traditional samosas can be a hassle to make at home, but with a surprising shortcut for the pastry shell, these samosas are much easier to make and will wow a crowd every time. If we're being honest, these do take longer than almost any other recipe in this book, but they are worth it! Plus, check out the tip below for getting the most out of your investment of time.

Ingredients

8   cups of vegetable oil (or enough for deep frying)
1   large onion
$^1/_2$ teaspoon of coriander seeds
$^1/_2$ teaspoon of cumin seeds
$^1/_2$ cup of frozen peas
1   15-ounce can of diced potatoes
$^1/_2$ teaspoon of salt
$^1/_4$ teaspoon of turmeric powder
$^1/_4$ teaspoon of red pepper powder
$^1/_4$ teaspoon of sugar
3   teaspoons of lemon juice (bottled or fresh)
3   tablespoons of all-purpose flour
4   large soft flour tortillas (I use the large 10-inch burrito-style tortillas)

Steps

1   Make the filling: Heat 1 tablespoon of oil in a medium pot over medium heat. While the oil is heating, chop the onion. Add the coriander and cumin seeds to the hot oil, followed by the onion. Cook the onion for about 5 minutes, stirring intermittently. Stir in the peas, drained potatoes, and the next 4 ingredients and cook, covered, for another 5 minutes. Remove from heat and add the lemon juice. With a potato smasher or fork, mash up the mixture a bit so it is scoopable but not completely mashed. Set the potato mixture aside.

2   Prep the oil: In a large pot over medium-high heat on the back burner, add about 8 cups of oil for deep frying. (Or use a deep fryer if you have one.) The exact amount of oil will depend on the size of your pot, but you basically want enough oil so that your samosas will be fully immersed while frying, but the pot should be no more than half full. Allow the oil to slowly heat as you move on to steps 3 and 4. (You want the oil to stay right around 350°F.)

3   Make your glue: In a small bowl, mix together the flour with about 3 tablespoons of water to form a paste. You may need to add a little more flour or water, but basically you want a sticky texture to bind your samosas shut.

4   Assemble the samosas: Cut 4 soft flour tortillas into quarters, yielding 16 pieces. Make the samosas as follows:

First, take a quarter piece with the rounded edge positioned closest to you. Scoop 1 heaping tablespoon of the potato filling into the center.

Second, fold the right bottom corner of the tortilla over the filling.

Third, use your fingers to place some of the flour glue along the bottom rounded edge of the left corner and then fold the left bottom corner over the potato filling. Press gently to seal.

Fourth, add glue to the top corner and fold it over to make a sealed-triangular piece. After you've assembled 8 samosas, the oil should be ready.

5   Fry the samosas: Check if the oil is ready by tearing off a small piece of leftover flour tortilla and dropping it into the oil. If the tortilla quickly rises to the surface and begins to sizzle, then the oil is ready. If the tortilla turns brown right away, the oil is too hot. (You want to keep the oil at 350°F.) When the oil is ready, use metal tongs to carefully place the samosas in the oil, turning them when one side becomes golden brown. Once both sides are lightly browned, remove the samosa from the oil and drain on paper towels. You can continue to assemble the remaining samosas while the first batch fries. You should get about 16 samosas.

Serves 4.

Serve plain or with tamarind dipping sauce, raita, or ketchup. Samosas are best served immediately, but they can be refrigerated for several days and reheated in the oven or toaster.

Tip: Be efficient and make a double or triple batch! You can freeze the unfried, assembled samosas for a few months. Just defrost them and then fry, per the recipe.

"Beef" Samosas *in 50 minutes*

This samosa variation uses a faux beef filling. On the outside, they look the same as potato samosas, but the beefy-ginger filling gives this version an unmistakable character of its own. I have a hard time making one version without the other.

Ingredients

8	cups of vegetable oil (enough for deep frying)
1	large onion
$1/2$	teaspoon of coriander seeds
$1/2$	teaspoon of cumin seeds
$2/3$	cup of frozen peas
$1^1/2$	cups of faux ground beef or meatless crumbles
$1/2$	teaspoon of salt
$1/4$	teaspoon of red pepper powder
1	teaspoon of curry powder
1	teaspoon of ground ginger powder or paste
3	tablespoons of all-purpose flour
4	large soft flour tortillas (I use the large 10-inch burrito-style tortillas)

Steps

1   Make the filling: Heat 1 tablespoon of oil in a medium pot over medium heat. Meanwhile, chop the onion. Add the coriander and cumin seeds to the hot oil and add the onion 30 seconds later. Cook the onion for about 5 minutes. Stir in the peas, faux ground beef, and the next 4 ingredients. Cover and cook for another 5 minutes. Remove this filling from the heat and set aside.

2   Using this "beef" filling in place of the potato filling, continue making the samosas following steps 2 – 5 from the preceding "Potato Samosa" recipe.

Serves 4.

Tandoori Skewers *in 35 minutes*

Ingredients

8-12 long wooden or metal skewers

1	teaspoon of red pepper powder
$1/2$	teaspoon of cumin powder
$1/2$	teaspoon of salt
$1/2$	teaspoon of garlic powder
$1/4$	teaspoon of ginger powder
$1/4$	teaspoon of ground cardamom
2	tablespoons of lemon juice (bottled or fresh)
3	tablespoons of plain yogurt
1	large bell pepper (any color)
1	onion
6-8	button mushrooms
1	12-ounce package of extra-firm tofu, paneer, or meat substitute of your choice
$1/4$	cup of olive oil (if using skillet-cooking method)

Steps

1   If you are using wooden skewers, place them in a glass of water to soak as you prepare the food so that they won't burn while grilling. Stir together the first eight listed food ingredients into a tandoori paste.

2   Cut the bell pepper, onion, mushrooms, and tofu/faux meat into large homogenous chunks or cubes. (If you are using tofu, drain it and pat dry with a towel before cutting it.) Place the bell peppers, onions, and mushrooms in a microwavable dish; cover and microwave for about 2 minutes to soften.

3   Assemble the skewers by threading a chunk of bell pepper, onion, mushroom and uncooked tofu/faux meat onto each skewer. Lightly brush the vegetables and tofu with the tandoori paste.

4   You can cook the skewers in one of several ways. You can cook them on an actual outdoor grill, or in a bit of olive oil in an indoor grill pan or skillet—this takes about 4-8 minutes per side until the vegetables are tender. You can also cook them directly over the gas burner on your range top: remove the grate; line the burner with aluminum foil (for easy clean up); and then carefully roast 2 skewers at a time directly above or in the flame, rotating when the edges of the vegetables and tofu start to blacken. After about 2-3 minutes, the vegetables should be cooked. This cooking method is fast and gives your vegetables a smoky taste while still maintaining their crunch.

Serves 2-4.

Palak Paneer Salad *in 30 minutes*

Ingredients

2	tablespoons of lemon juice
5	tablespoons of bottled curry sauce (*e.g.*, tikka masala curry cooking sauce)
3	tablespoons of olive oil
1	small onion
1	yellow or orange bell pepper
4	ounces of paneer cheese (you can also use fresh mozzarella or tofu)
1	cup of cherry tomatoes
6	ounces of fresh spinach
$1/3$	cup of cilantro leaves
$1/4$	cup of mint leaves
1	teaspoon of coarse or regular table salt
$1/8$	teaspoon of black pepper (just a pinch)

Steps

1   Make the dressing: In a large salad bowl, stir together the lemon juice with 3 tablespoons of the curry sauce, 2 tablespoons of oil, and 1 tablespoon of water.

2   Thinly slice the onion and bell pepper and toss them into the dressing to marinate.

3   Cut the paneer (or mozzarella or tofu) into bite-sized cubes and halve the cherry tomatoes. (If you are using fresh mozzarella as a substitute, add it straight to your dressing and only fry up the tomatoes as described next.) Add 1 tablespoon of oil to a large skillet over medium heat. After about 1 minute, toss in the paneer or tofu with 2 tablespoon of the curry sauce and $1/2$ teaspoon of salt. Cook for 3-5 minutes or until the paneer/tofu is lightly browned. Add the tomatoes to the pan and cook it with the cheese for 1 more minute. Remove the tomatoes and paneer from the skillet and add them to the curry dressing.

4   Roughly chop or tear the spinach, cilantro, and mint leaves. Toss the greens with the dressing, veggies, cheese, and the remaining $1/2$ teaspoon of salt and a pinch of pepper.

Serves 2-4.

Serve immediately after dressing the salad.

I have to admit that a lot of Indian food can be characterized as "mushy." As much as I love a hot curry, I sometimes wish I could have all the Indian flavors I crave in a lighter, crispier medium. That's why I created this salad version of palak paneer. It gives you the best of both worlds and will not weigh you down.

Tip: Steps 1-3 can be done up to a day in advance. Just refrigerate the marinated ingredients until you're ready to toss in the greens!

Chaat Salad *in 25 minutes*

Ingredients

1	sheet of thawed puff pastry (about 10" X 10")
1	can of tamarind nectar/juice (you can find an 11 or 12-ounce can in the international food aisle)
1	15-ounce can of diced potatoes
1	15.5-ounce can of chickpeas
1	small red onion
1	large tomato
1	large handful of fresh cilantro (about $1/2$ a cup)
$1/2$	cup of plain yogurt
$1/2$	teaspoon of coarse or regular table salt
$1/8$	teaspoon of black pepper (a pinch)

Steps

1   Roll out the puff pastry onto a lightly-greased cookie sheet and cut it into squares (4" squares are good). Bake according to the package's instructions, adding an extra 5 minutes so that the pastry is light brown and crispy (baking for around 20 minutes total). Meanwhile, move to step 2.

2   Pour the full can of tamarind nectar into a small saucepan and bring it to a boil. Boil, uncovered, for 10-12 minutes or until the nectar has condensed into a thin syrup (this will be your tamarind dressing). While the dressing is simmering, move to steps 3 and 4.

3   Drain the potatoes and chickpeas; empty them into a microwave-safe bowl; and microwave for 1-2 minutes.

4   Finely chop the onion (you want about $2/3$ cup). Roughly chop the tomato and cilantro.

5   Assemble the chaat salad: Once the puff pastry has baked, pull the pastry apart into thin crispy squares (if desired, pull apart each of the squares into 2 thinner layers or just use the squares as is, and slightly smash in the center so that the toppings don't roll off). Top each square with the potatoes, chickpeas, onions, tomatoes, and cilantro. Generously drizzle with the tamarind dressing and yogurt and sprinkle on salt and pepper.

Serves 2-4.

"Chaats" are savory snacks that are very popular Indian street food. The first time I had chaat, I instantly fell in love with what I dubbed the "Indian taco." It was a perfect combination of potatoes, chickpeas, and onions in a crunchy dough cup, drizzled with chutneys—sweet, salt, and spice, all in one bite. I had to recreate the experience, but with some twists. Frozen puff pastry makes an effortless crunchy base. I've also streamlined the toppings, so there's less prep. The result is this healthier chaat salad—a perfect light appetizer or lunch.

Easy Entertaining: "Exotic Happy Hour"

Nothing inspires me to cook more than cooking for others. Of course, there's pleasure in making a wonderful meal for yourself, but for me that joy is multiplied when someone asks for seconds or maybe even a little doggy bag. There's nothing wrong with taking a little pride in your work!

I started entertaining (or trying to) as soon as I got an apartment in college. It was never anything fancy, mind you, but it was one of the first social experiences that I could cultivate on my own without a lot of money, and it made me feel like an adult. Though most of the meals were learning experiences, each one was special because it was shared.

One of my first victims was my boyfriend (now husband). Early on in our relationship, I decided to make him a spaghetti dinner with homemade marinara sauce. He ate it all, downing three tall glasses of water along the way. By his fourth glass of water, I was pretty sure that either he was diabetic or the food wasn't quite right. He later confessed that the marinara sauce was a tad spicy for his taste. Okay, his exact words might have been, "wasn't that just salsa you used for the spaghetti sauce?" But I like to remember it differently. It would be several years before I tried making homemade marinara sauce again. On the bright side, that was when I realized that my penchant for adding onions and lots of crushed red pepper flakes to everything was best channeled into cooking Indian food. Whether I was cooking curry for my college friends or making samosas for the office, I've tried to remember not to let modest resources, limited time, or perfectionism prevent me from sharing new food experiences with good people.

If you can make a few of the recipes in this chapter, then you can start entertaining today. Host your own "Wine & Chutney" party! You'll get all the credit for cooking, without actually making a full dinner. Just follow these tips.

Be Familiar
With the food, that is—what you do with your company is your business! Just don't make them the guinea pigs. Be familiar enough with the recipe and what you're making so that you don't hit a last-minute snag and surprise your guests with a Bridget Jones-like blue soup.

Plan Ahead, Most of the Time

I love entertaining, but it can become overwhelming if you're not careful. If you're pressed for time, it might seem counterintuitive to have to plan out a party in your free moments. But if you're going to have several guests, then it pays to strategize. If you can, think about what you're going to make a week in advance and then make everything that can be made ahead of time when you have pockets of free time. You can always make a few chutneys a couple of days before your gathering or prepare samosas weeks in advance and keep them frozen.

On the other hand . . . a little spontaneity can be charming. One of my most memorable cooking experiences was when I invited a few friends over after work for appetizers and we ended up inventing our own cocktails out of ice cream and an old bottle of vodka because we ran out of wine. (Check out the Desserts chapter for these drinks!) The good news is that there are some quick recipes in this chapter that can be thrown together in the time it takes your friends to come over.

Keep it Simple

When my husband and I were newlyweds, I was very excited to host our first brunch. We were expecting a few of my husband's friends and I was eager to impress, so I tried to pull out all the stops with freshly squeezed juice, crepes, a frittata, and two salads. I was making some new dishes and severely underestimated the time it would take to make everything that morning. With each nervous glance at the clock, our tiny kitchen was getting hotter and even smaller. I was in the homestretch, battling it out with the pit of a mango, when I let the knife slip and sliced my finger. Something about the heat, the amount of blood gushing into the sink, and the fact that I hadn't eaten all day caused me to faint, right there, next to the refrigerator. This time it was my husband's turn to wonder whether I was diabetic. I was still a bit dazed when our friends arrived but took comfort in the fact that we had a good story to serve in lieu of the salad.

So, whatever you do, don't overdo. Pair one or two complicated items with a few quick ones and take help from store-bought goodies. Don't worry about keeping it simple. If your guests are still hungry and chatty once the chutneys run out, just order take-out or move the party to the closest restaurant for a nice dinner to round out the evening. And if you do want to go big with a lot of different appetizers, chutneys, and drinks, that's great, but you'll just have to plan ahead that much more.

Sample Happy Hour Menus

1. Simple and Sophisticated (lighter fare)
Chaat salad
Mango chutney & pita chips
1 soft cheese & 1 hard cheese with grapes
Wine (white or rosé)

Tips: Make the chutney a day or two ahead of time. The chaat should be made fresh, although you can make the tamarind dressing in advance.

2. Just Wine and Chutneys (lighter fare)
Mango chutney
Tomato chutney
Coconut chutney
Cilantro chutney
Store-bought dippers: warm chunks of ciabatta or other crusty bread, kettle chips, whole wheat crackers, endives, cucumbers, and peppers.
Wine (red or white)

Tips: You can make all the chutneys a day or so in advance. Have your guests pair different wines with chutneys, as you would with cheese.

3. TV Watching Happy Hour (medium fare)

Veggie fritters & tomato chutney
Lemon cilantro dip & store-bought hummus with warm pita chunks
White wine or beer
Mango creamsicles (see Desserts)

Tips: This is a fun menu if you're inviting friends over to watch your favorite show or a game. Make the lemon cilantro dip and tomato chutney a day in advance. Make the veggie fritters right before guests arrive. Make the mango creamsicles later in the evening. For a larger crowd, you can add spinach pakoras to the menu—just fry them in the same oil in which you fried the veggie fritters.

4. Indian Summer Soiree (heavier fare)

Tandoori tofu skewers
Onion-spiced raita with kettle chips
Lemon cilantro dip with tortilla chips
Potato or beef samosas with tamarind dipping sauce
Indian beer or sangria

Tips: Assemble and freeze the unfried samosas ahead of time. Make the lemon cilantro dip and tamarind dipping sauce a day in advance. Do the prep work for the skewers—including making the tandoori paste and chopping the veggies—a day or a few hours in advance. Before guests arrive, defrost and fry the samosas, assemble and cook the skewers, and make the raita. And don't be shy, ask early arrivals to help assemble skewers or assign deep-frying duties to your braver friends. They'll likely enjoy the food even more if they have a hand in making it . . . at least that's what people say. Regardless, it takes the pressure off when there's another cook in the kitchen!

CURRIES IN A HURRY

Rich curries like saag paneer and kormas usually dominate the menus of Indian restaurants in the United States. While these saucy entrees really hit the spot, they can seem quite mysterious and intimidating to make at home. But you actually can make these and other vegetable curries, and you can make them in a hurry. Any night of the week, you can have Indian curry without dealing with a fancy restaurant, questionable service, or prepackaged items that barely feed one. The recipes in this chapter are super simple and use healthy ingredients like ground nut butters, canned tomatoes, and yogurt for their curry base. These recipes take about half an hour or less, and each one makes a great quick meal with rice or flatbread. So check your email, pour yourself a glass, and let's get cooking!

No-Chop Veggie Korma

"Chicken" Korma

Palak Tofu

Saag "Chicken"

Matar Tofu

Egg Curry

Tangy Chickpea Curry

Potato Curry

Corn Curry

Quick Cauliflower Curry

Roasted Bell Pepper Curry

Yellow Potato & Mustard Seed Curry

"Meaty" Curries and the Lessons of Childhood

When I first saw that the stores were selling ground nut butters of the non-peanut variety, I flipped out. The cooking possibilities were endless. It was like I was a kid again.

When I actually was a kid, I had a similar moment of excitement about regular old butter. It was my first day of first grade and I got to be at school for the whole day and eat in the cafeteria like a big kid. There, on my plastic tray next to a foil container full of macaroni and cheese and mashed potatoes was my bread and butter. (It was the 80s in Ohio—carbs were in.) Of course, I'd had butter before, but my six-year-old eyes had never seen the cafeteria version of a single-serving of butter. It was so intricately packaged. The pad of butter was neatly nestled between a small square of white cardboard and a square of wax paper on which the word "butter" was repeated in precious blue script. I was about to peel back the paper, but I stopped myself. This was too good to eat right then and there.

I had to show somebody the sophisticated delicacies that this public school was offering. Naturally, I put the designer butter in my pocket so that I could show my mom when I got home. And we all know what happened. Hours later, in our living room, I remembered the little gift tucked away in my corduroys. "Mommy! Mommy! I brought you something from school—look!" I pulled out the remains of a greasy piece of wax paper. My pocket was permanently stained but I learned my first lesson in food. Butter melts!

Well, who says you can't be a kid again? Realizing that I could just spoon out some cashew or almond nut butter from a jar and quickly melt it into a creamy and delicious curry was one of my most exciting cooking experiences. And like my discovery in the cafeteria, I for sure had to tell somebody. So here I am, telling you. Pockets intact.

Many Indian curries, particularly North Indian dishes like kormas, are made of rich, nut-based sauces that contain ground cashews or other nuts. And a lot of the traditional recipes for these dishes require blanching, boiling, and grinding nuts into a paste . . . have I lost you yet? Just thinking about a recipe like that stresses me out. But with ground nut butters, most of the hard work is done for you. You can cut down the time of making these rich meat-like dishes without losing the healthy protein kick you'd otherwise get from using fresh nuts. And just so there's no confusion, despite the name, these nut butters don't actually contain any butter or dairy—they're just ground nuts, so they're not as indulgent as they sound. Many of the curries that follow use a healthy serving of nut butter, along with other easy-to-use ingredients like yogurt, store-bought pureed ginger paste and canned tomatoes—all which help form a delicious and fragrant curry sauce in minutes.

I hope you find one you like. And who knows, maybe you'll even get the urge to share your discovery with someone you love.

No-Chop Veggie Korma *in 20 minutes*

This curry takes easy to the next level. It's wholesome and healthy and it's entirely made from ingredients in your freezer and cupboard. Demanding boss? Family drama? Just too much to juggle? Whatever else is going on in your life, this one-pot, no-chop dinner won't let you down.

Ingredients

3–4 cups of frozen vegetables (standard mixed vegetables work fine!)
1   14.5-ounce can of diced or sliced potatoes (drained)
1   cup of coconut milk
1   cup of canned diced tomatoes or tomato sauce
2   tablespoons of cashew nut or almond butter
1   tablespoon of garam masala powder
1   tablespoon of curry powder
$^1/_2$ teaspoon of red pepper powder
1   teaspoon of salt

Steps

Combine all the ingredients in a medium pot over medium heat. Stir well, cover, and cook for about 15 minutes, or until the vegetables are fully cooked through. (Intermittently stir the curry while it cooks.)

Serves 2-4.

Goes well with plain rice or coconut peanut rice.

"Chicken" Korma *in 30 minutes*

This curry has universal appeal and really hits the spot if you ever do crave meat. The "faux" chicken is not only vegetarian, but it cooks up in no time!

Ingredients

1	tablespoon of oil
1	yellow onion
1	tablespoon of minced garlic (bottled or fresh)
1	teaspoon of ginger paste or powder
1	8-ounce packet of frozen meatless "chicken"
	(*e.g.*, meatless chicken strips from Morningstar Farms or Beyond Meat)
1	14.5-ounce can of diced tomatoes
2	tablespoons of cashew nut or almond butter
1	tablespoon of curry powder
1	teaspoon of garam masala powder
$1/2$	teaspoon of red pepper powder
1	teaspoon of salt
2-4	tablespoons of yogurt, heavy cream, or coconut cream
1	handful of cilantro for garnishing (optional)

Steps

1   Add the oil to a medium pot over medium heat. Thinly slice the onion and add it, the garlic, and the ginger to the hot oil, then toss. Roughly chop the meatless chicken into large chunks and add it to the pot. Cook, uncovered, for about 3-4 minutes, tossing intermittently.

2   Once the onion and chicken are slightly browned, add all the remaining ingredients to the pot, except for the yogurt and cilantro. Then add $1/4$ cup of water and stir thoroughly. Cover and cook, stirring intermittently. (Add 1-2 more tablespoons of water as needed to prevent the sauce from drying out.)

3   After the korma has cooked for about 8 minutes, remove from heat, and stir in the yogurt or cream, to taste. Roughly chop or tear the cilantro (if using), and stir it in.

Serves 2-4.

Serve over rice, naan, or bread.

Palak Tofu *in 25 minutes*

Ingredients

2	tablespoons of butter or olive oil
1	12-ounce package of extra-firm tofu
$^2/_3$	cup of milk or coconut milk
1	tablespoon of curry powder
1	teaspoon of garam masala powder
$^1/_4$	teaspoon of red pepper powder
$^2/_3$	teaspoon of salt
2	tablespoons of cashew nut or almond butter
1	10-12-ounce bag of spinach (or a 10-ounce box of frozen chopped spinach)

Steps

1   Add the butter to a medium pan over medium-high heat. Place the tofu block on a cutting board, and using a kitchen towel, gently press out the excess water. Cut the tofu into bite-sized cubes. Place the cubes in the hot butter and fry for about 7-10 minutes or until browned. (Do not continuously stir while browning or the cubes will crumble; just flip them over once or twice while cooking). While the tofu is frying, move to step 2.

2   In a separate medium pot over medium heat, combine the remaining ingredients, except the fresh spinach (but if you are using frozen spinach, add it now). Stir in $^1/_2$ cup of water and cook, uncovered, for about 5 minutes. Then, if you are using fresh spinach, gently fold the leaves directly into this boiling broth. Cook for 3 more minutes. (Optional: If you prefer a smooth, restaurant-style texture, you can blend this cooked spinach mixture now—an immersion blender works particularly well here.)

3   Fold the fried tofu into the spinach mixture and simmer together for another 3-4 minutes.

Serves 2-4.

Eat over plain rice, or a lightly flavored pilaf like lemon rice.

Tip: Turn this into an easy "Aloo Saag." Just skip step 1 and swap in diced cooked potatoes for the tofu in step 3. (A microwaved baked potato or canned diced potatoes works fine!)

Saag "Chicken" *in 25 minutes*

This is my version of a chicken salad sandwich, and it's a quick way of getting diverse greens into your diet.

Ingredients

1	10-ounce package of frozen greens (*e.g.* collard, kale, or mustard greens)
2	tablespoons of cashew nut or almond butter
1	cup of plain yogurt
1	tablespoon of curry powder
1	teaspoon of garam masala powder
$^1/_2$	teaspoon of red pepper powder
1	teaspoon of salt
1	cup of frozen meatless "chicken"
	(*e.g.*, meatless chicken strips from Morningstar Farms or Beyond Meat)

Steps

1   Thaw and slightly cook the frozen greens in the microwave on high for about 3-5 minutes. Meanwhile, move to step 2.

2   In a medium pot over medium heat, combine all the remaining ingredients, except the meatless chicken, and stir. Drain the thawed greens and add them to the pot. Cover and cook this saag sauce for 7-10 minutes.

3   Roughly chop the frozen meatless chicken and add it into the saag sauce. Stir, cover, and simmer together for about 5 more minutes. (If the sauce become too dry, stir in a few tablespoons of water.)

Serves 2-4.

Best with pita, naan, or whole wheat flour tortillas.

Matar Tofu *in 20 minutes*

Matar paneer is a North Indian favorite, but homemade paneer takes a while to make, so I usually leave that for the restaurants and use tofu instead. I always have a package of tofu in the fridge, which means I can make this dish any night of the week, even if I'm running low on fresh veggies!

Ingredients

1	14.5-ounce can of diced tomatoes
3	tablespoons of tomato paste
1	tablespoon of minced garlic (bottled or fresh)
1	teaspoon of ginger paste or powder
1	teaspoon of curry powder
$1/2$	teaspoon of garam masala powder
$1/2$	teaspoon of red pepper powder
1	teaspoon of salt
$1/2$	teaspoon of sugar or honey
2	tablespoons of cashew nut or almond butter
$1^1/_2$	cups of frozen peas
2	tablespoons of butter or olive oil
1	12-ounce package of extra-firm tofu
$1/4$	cup of milk or nut/oat milk

Steps

1   Stir in all but the last three ingredients into a medium pot over medium heat and cover. As this tomato sauce cooks, move to step 2.

2   Place the butter in a medium pan over medium-high heat. Place the tofu block on a cutting board, and using a kitchen towel, gently press out the excess water. Cut the tofu into bite-sized cubes. Place the cubes in the hot butter and fry for about 7-10 minutes or until browned. (Do not continuously stir the cubes while browning or they will crumble; just flip them over once or twice while cooking.)

3   Reduce the heat under the tomato sauce mixture to a low simmer. Stir in the milk and then gently fold in the browned tofu and cook together for another minute or so.

Serves 2-4.

Best with rice, naan, or pita bread.

Egg Curry *in 35 minutes*

This curry is slightly more involved than the others in this chapter, but the fried boiled eggs make for a unique dish that is very filling for vegetarians and meat eaters alike.

Ingredients

4	eggs
2	medium onions
2	tablespoons of oil
1	teaspoon of coriander seeds
1	teaspoon of black mustard seeds
1	teaspoon of cumin seeds
1	tablespoon of minced garlic (bottled or fresh)
$^1/_2$	teaspoon of ginger paste or powder
$^1/_2$	teaspoon of crushed red pepper flakes
1	14.5-ounce can of crushed or diced tomatoes
1	teaspoon of salt
2	teaspoons of curry powder
2	tablespoons of cream (optional)

Steps

1 *Boil the eggs*: Place the eggs in cold water in a medium pot and cook over high heat. Once the water reaches a rolling boil, turn off the heat. Cover and leave the eggs in this hot water for about 10 minutes. Meanwhile, move to step 2.

2 *Make the sauce:* Chop the onions. Heat 1 tablespoon of oil in a separate medium pot over medium heat for about 45 seconds and then add the coriander, mustard, and cumin seeds to the oil. Once one or two mustard seeds start popping, add the onion, garlic, ginger, and red pepper flakes. Toss, cover, and cook for about 5 minutes. Then, stir in the canned tomatoes, salt, and curry powder. Let this sauce simmer over low heat while you move to step 3.

3 *Fry the eggs:* Peel the eggs under cold running water. Heat 1 tablespoon of oil in a medium pan for about 45 seconds. Fry the whole eggs in the pan until they develop a golden brown coating. Careful—the eggs may start to make a popping noise and the oil may sputter. Keep tossing the eggs gently in the oil so that they brown evenly.

4   *Finisher:* For a creamier curry, slightly blend the tomato sauce using a regular or immersion blender (this step is optional). If desired, stir the cream into the tomato sauce (add more for a milder flavor). Gently fold the fried eggs into the tomato sauce and serve.

Serves 2-4.

Eat over plain rice or with pita or crusty bread.

Veggie Curries for College and for Life

I had this awesome friend in college who shared my meat-free diet. He was a straight-edge computer science major in a punk rock band who was on the debate team with me and lived two houses down. You've got to love college. He wanted to eat healthier; I wanted to save up for summer rent. So we came up with an arrangement—every other Sunday we'd drive out to the grocery store like an old married couple. He'd pay for most of the groceries and I'd take them home and cook elaborate (by college standards) meals for the both of us.

Every few days, I'd deliver the dinners to my friend like a dedicated meals-on-wheels professional, except for a different kind of senior. Sure, my friend's roommates might have thought it was weird when this girl showed up in sweatpants on a Friday night to drop off a stack of containers full of curries and rice, while the sounds of drums reverberated through their house, but we had a deal!

Between school, multiple part-time jobs, and figuring out what we wanted to be when we grew up, we couldn't juggle a lot of fresh vegetables. So, we'd typically stock up on frozen or canned veggies. A meal would center on chickpeas or potatoes and there were often lots of onions and canned tomatoes involved.

That was the year I first started making many of the curries that follow. Chickpea curry was one of our favorites because it was tasty, full of protein, and the ingredients were cheap. We'd eat it over rice, couscous, in a burrito, or in a pita with cauliflower curry and lettuce. Potato curries were up there too, and if we were really being fancy, we'd eat them in real dishes instead of out of Tupperware.

These curries were versatile enough that I could always change things up and throw in some extra veggies like carrots, spinach, or peas. It was a good year. I got to cook, stay in my awesome apartment for one last summer, and my friend got to sneak in a little more band practice. Best of all, we both ate our veggies! May these curries work similar wonders for you.

Chickpea and cauliflower curries over pita, topped with lettuce and a drizzle of yogurt.

Tangy Chickpea Curry *in 30 minutes*

Ingredients

1	tablespoon of oil
1	large onion
2	tablespoons of minced garlic
$1^1/_2$	teaspoons of ginger paste or powder
1	tablespoon of curry powder
2	teaspoons of cumin powder
$^1/_4$	teaspoon of red pepper powder
1	teaspoon of salt
3	tablespoons of tomato paste
1	14.5-ounce can of diced tomatoes
1	15.5-ounce can of chickpeas/garbanzo beans (drained)
1	handful of cilantro (optional)

Steps

1   Heat the oil in a medium pot over medium heat. Meanwhile, chop the onion and then add it to the hot oil along with the garlic. Toss and cook for about 5 minutes.

2   When the onion has just started to brown, add in the ginger, curry powder, cumin powder, red pepper powder, salt, tomato paste, and the canned tomatoes. Stir and slightly mash the tomatoes with a fork or potato masher. Then add the chickpeas and thoroughly stir and cover. Simmer together on medium-low heat for about 7-10 minutes, stirring occasionally. When the curry is thick and saucy, remove from heat. Roughly chop or tear the cilantro (if using) and stir it in.

Serves 2-4.

Tip: For a healthy boost of greens, stir in 2 cups of fresh kale, swiss chard, or spinach when you add the chickpeas.

Potato Curry *in 25 minutes*

For me, the plump raisins are the hidden gems of this sweet and aromatic dish, which you can make any night of the week, thanks to steam-in-bag potatoes.

Ingredients

1	package of steam-in-bag potatoes (1.5 lbs of fingerling or red potatoes)
2	tablespoons of oil
1	onion
1	teaspoon of salt
1	teaspoon of garam masala powder
1	teaspoon of curry powder
1/4	teaspoon of turmeric
2	tablespoons of tomato paste or ketchup
1/4	cup of raisins (I like golden raisins for this recipe)
1/4	teaspoon of honey or brown sugar

Steps

1   Cook the steam-in-bag potatoes in the microwave according to the package's directions, but for 1 minute less than instructed. Meanwhile, move to step 2.

2   Add 1 tablespoon of oil to a medium pot over medium heat. Chop the onion and add it to the saucepan. Toss, cover, and cook for about 2-3 minutes, stirring intermittently. Stir in all the remaining ingredients and 1 cup of water and bring this sauce to a simmer. (You want this to cook down to a thin gravy—it'll take about 7-10 minutes.)

3   Once the potatoes are done, add 1 tablespoon of oil to a large pan over medium-high heat. Carefully remove the cooked potatoes from their steam-in-bag and cut them into 1/2-inch-thick discs. Place each slice in the hot oil. Cook each side just until the potatoes develop a nice roasted crust. Gently add the potatoes to the saucy gravy.

Serves 2-4.

Tip: Swap in sweet potatoes, yams, or pumpkin for variety and a great Thanksgiving side dish!

Corn Curry *in 25 minutes*

Ingredients

3	ears of corn in their husks (or 3 cups of frozen corn kernels)
1	tablespoon of oil
1	onion
$^1/_2$	teaspoon of cumin seeds
2	teaspoons of minced garlic (bottled or fresh)
1	teaspoon of ginger paste or powder
$^1/_2$	teaspoon of turmeric powder
$^1/_2$	teaspoon of red pepper powder
1	teaspoon of salt
1	cup of plain yogurt
1	handful of cilantro (optional)

Steps

1   Place the ears of corn in the microwave with the husks intact; cook on high for 4-5 minutes. By leaving the corn in their husks, they will cook in their own moisture. (Alternatively, you can cook frozen corn according to the package's directions.) After the corn has cooked, allow the ears to cool in their husks for about 5 minutes. While the corn is cooking, move to step 2.

2   Add the oil to a medium pot over medium heat. Roughly chop the onion and add it, the cumin seeds, garlic, and ginger to the pot. Toss, cover, and cook for about 5 minutes and then add the turmeric, red pepper powder, and salt. Cook for 2-3 more minutes or until the onion is tender. Add the yogurt to this mixture and blend until the onion is ground. (An immersion blender works well, but you can also transfer the mixture into a regular blender.)

3   Once the corn has cooled, remove the ears from their husks and silk. (Do this directly over a trash can, so there's no cleanup!) Shuck the corn kernels with a knife and add them to the onion mixture. (Or, for a Mexican street corn alternative, simply spoon the onion mixture over the corn on the cob.) Roughly chop or tear the cilantro leaves and sprinkle over the curry if desired.

Serves 2-4.

Eat plain or with rice.

Quick Cauliflower Curry *in 25 minutes*

Ingredients

1	16-ounce bag of frozen cauliflower
1	tablespoon of oil
$1/4$	teaspoon of cumin seeds
$1/2$	teaspoon of salt
$1/2$	teaspoon of red pepper powder
$1/4$	teaspoon of turmeric powder
$1/2$	teaspoon of curry powder
$1/4$	teaspoon of sugar
1	handful of chopped cilantro (optional)

Steps

1   Roughly chop the cauliflower florets so that you have smaller bite-size pieces. (It's not necessary to thaw the frozen cauliflower before chopping, but you may find it a bit easier to chop after it has been out of the freezer for about 5 minutes or microwaved for 30 seconds.)

2   Heat the oil in a large pan over medium heat; after about 45 seconds, add the cumin seeds. After another minute (before the cumin seeds darken), add the frozen cauliflower, salt, red pepper powder, turmeric, curry powder, and sugar. Toss and cover. Allow the cauliflower to cook until tender (about 10-15 minutes), tossing intermittently. If the cauliflower dries out before it is cooked, add water, a tablespoon at a time. Roughly chop or tear the cilantro and add it to the cauliflower, if desired.

Serves 2-4.

Serve hot over rice. This also pairs well with chickpea curry in a pita.

Roasted Bell Pepper Curry *in 25 minutes*

Ingredients

2   bell peppers (any variety or combination is fine)
1   tablespoon of oil
$1/_2$ teaspoon of cumin seeds
$1/_2$ teaspoon of black mustard seeds
1   teaspoon of salt
$1/_4$ cup of garbanzo bean/chickpea flour (found in natural food stores)
$1/_4$ teaspoon of red pepper powder
$1/_4$ teaspoon of cumin powder

Steps

1   Chop or slice the bell peppers into medium chunks. Add the oil to a medium pot over medium heat. After about 45 seconds, add the cumin and mustard seeds. Once one or two mustard seeds start popping, add the bell pepper and salt. Stir, cover, and cook for about 6 minutes, tossing intermittently. Meanwhile, move to step 2.

2   Combine the flour, red pepper powder, and cumin powder in a bowl and set aside.

3   After the bell peppers are tender (about 6-8 minutes), stir in the flour mixture along with $1/_4$ cup of water to partially coat the peppers. Reduce to low heat. Cover and cook for another 3-4 minutes. If the flour is too dry or begins to burn, stir in another $1/_4$ cup of water. The curry is done once the flour is no longer powdery and is golden brown and cooked through.

Serves 2-4.

Serve as a side dish alongside rice or lentils.

Yellow Potato & Mustard Seed Curry
in 20 minutes

Ingredients

1	small onion
1	teaspoon of oil
1	teaspoon of black mustard seeds
1/4	teaspoon of coriander seeds
1/4	teaspoon of cumin seeds
1/4	teaspoon of crushed red pepper flakes
1/4	teaspoon of ground turmeric
1	teaspoon of salt
1	14.5-ounce can of diced potatoes (drained)
2	tablespoons of lemon juice (bottled or fresh)

Steps

1   Add the oil to a small pot over medium heat. Chop the onion. After the oil has been heating for about 1 minute, add in the mustard, coriander, and cumin seeds. Once one or two mustard seeds start popping, add the onion and red pepper flakes to the pot. Cover and cook for about 5 minutes, stirring intermittently.

2   After the onions have been cooking for about 5 minutes, stir in the turmeric, salt, and diced potatoes. Cover and cook for another 5 minutes. Then, using a fork or potato smasher, slightly mash and mix the potatoes so that the curry is well blended. Stir in the lemon juice and remove from heat.

Serves 2-4.

This curry is traditionally eaten with dosas but can also be served over rice or in a wheat tortilla.

LAZY LENTILS & SOUPS

As a rich source of plant protein, lentils are the cornerstone of vegetarian cuisine in India. The wide variety of lentils is matched only by India's diverse use of them in its cooking. They can be boiled, fried, ground, and used in both savory and sweet dishes.

But for our purposes, the best thing about lentils is that you can prepare them quickly and they will still taste great. So when you're beat from a long day, I say let yourself be a little lazy! By sticking to a fast-cooking red lentil, using the right canned and frozen accompaniments, and knowing just when to use your microwave, this chapter will show you how to prepare lentils and soups with minimal effort.

Spinach Dal

Brown Butter & Spice Dal

Mango Dal

Tomato Dal

Sambar

Lemon Lentil Ginger Soup

Tomato Rasam

Spicy Lemon Rasam

Garlic Chickpea Soup

Pongal (Lentils with Rice)

Pongal Veggie Balls for Kids

Lazy Lentils: The Basics

What kind of lentils do I use?

Before we dive in, you should know that there are many kinds of lentils and they all cook a little differently. Like pasta, lentils can cook to different degrees of tenderness. Depending on how much water you add, some lentils will reach a texture of mashed potatoes or even soup.

Unless otherwise specified, you can use red lentils ("split masoor dal") or yellow lentils ("split pigeon peas" or "unoily toor dal") for the recipes that follow. Red lentils are widely available in regular grocery stores, and they cook up faster than yellow lentils. However, yellow lentils should not be ignored, as they have more protein and are a bit more substantial.

Red lentils (split masoor dal)   Yellow lentils (toor dal)

There are tons of other varieties, including brown lentils, white lentils ("urad dal"), little chickpeas ("chana dal"), and split mung beans ("moong dal"). Some of these are great to add to soups, while others are often soaked and ground in Indian cuisine to make savory crepe batter. But as a meal unto itself, the red and yellow lentils are our quickest bet. Curious about canned lentils? Check out page 95.

What do I need to know about cooking them?

Red lentils will be our default here, and the microwave method is by far my favorite way to cook them. But if you are making more than 1 cup of lentils or you want to cook yellow lentils, then a pressure cooker is the fastest method. I'll admit that it took me a long time to come around to the pressure cooker—mostly because my mom never used one when I was growing up, and I had heard stories that made it sound intimidating and even dangerous. But today, there are many safe and user-friendly options, so the pressure cooker is definitely something to consider if you cook lentils regularly. For our purposes, you can use your pressure cooker/instant pot to cook the lentils in all the recipes in this chapter— just follow the directions for your specific brand of pressure cooker.

Most of the lentil recipes call for half a cup of lentils. If you are using a large pressure cooker, you may want to cook at least 1 cup of lentils and just reserve half a cup, or you can double the recipe to accommodate a full cup. Although you should follow the directions for your type of pressure cooker, I've generally found the following guidelines useful:

> For yellow lentils: Use 1 cup of lentils, $2^1/_2$ - 3 cups of water, and cook for about 15 minutes (3 whistles) or use the manual/pressure cooking setting on the instant pot (this should take about 12 minutes).

> For red lentils: If you're cooking 1 cup or less, the stovetop or microwave may be just as easy. But for larger quantities, use 1 part lentils to 2 parts water and cook for about 6-10 minutes (1-2 whistles), or use the manual/pressure cooking setting on the instant pot (this should take about 7 minutes).

For non-pressure cooking, I recommend sticking with red lentils in the beginning. They cook up very fast using the microwave or stove. Yellow lentils take a little longer to get to an al dente stage and much longer (over 40 minutes!) to get to a delicious creamy texture by conventional boiling. So if you like your dal creamy and smooth (which is how it's generally eaten in India), I recommend only using red lentils or get a pressure cooker. And just so you know, another option is to pre-soak your yellow lentils overnight, which will speed up the conventional cooking process.

But if you're like me, and all this talk about overnight soaking and complicated pressure cooking has deflated your enthusiasm, I've got just the thing: lazy lentils! On the next page you'll find some basic and low maintenance cooking methods for making quick lentils that you can use for all the recipes in this chapter. While I've included recipes for stovetop and yellow lentils, Lazy Lentils Recipe #1 is my go-to method— it's the quickest and the laziest cooking style!

Lazy Lentil Recipes

Lazy Lentils Recipe #1
Red Lentils in the Microwave (15 min)

In a large glass microwavable bowl (I use a 4-quart mixing bowl), combine $1/2$ cup of red lentils with 1 $1/2$ cups of water (i.e., 1 part lentils to 3 parts water). Cook for about 14 minutes in the microwave, uncovered. Carefully remove the hot bowl from the microwave and give it a stir. If you find it to be dry or flaky, stir in a tablespoon or so of water and it should be good to go.

Lazy Lentils Recipe #2
Red Lentils on the Stove (20-25 min)

In a large pot (at least 3 quarts), combine $1/2$ cup of red lentils with 1 $1/2$ cups of water. Cook, uncovered, on medium heat for about 10-15 minutes, keeping an eye on it to make sure it does not bubble over. (If you use a large pot and stir occasionally, this shouldn't happen.) After 10 minutes, when the water is no longer foaming and is largely soaked up by the lentils, add another $1/2$ cup of water; reduce to medium-low heat and cook for 10 minutes more, partially covering the pot. If the lentils dry out during the cooking process, add another $1/2$ cup of water and keep cooking. They should reach a fully cooked consistency after a total of 20-25 minutes.

Lazy Lentils Recipe #3
Yellow Lentils in the Microwave* (25-30 min)

In a large glass microwavable bowl (I use a 4-quart mixing bowl), combine $1/2$ cup of yellow lentils with $2 1/2$ cups of water (i.e., 1 part lentils to 5 parts water). Cook for about 25 minutes in the microwave, uncovered. Carefully remove the hot bowl from the microwave and give it a stir. If you find the lentils to be dry or flaky, stir in a tablespoon or so of water. Then, use a potato smasher or the back of a spoon to vigorously mash the lentils to break them up a bit. At this point, if you prefer a smoother consistency, add $1/4$ cup more of water and microwave for another 5 minutes.

*Note that yellow lentils take a bit longer to cook than red lentils, so if you want to make them in the microwave, you should expect them to be fairly al dente or expect to be using the microwave for a long time.

Lazy Lentils Recipe #4
Yellow Lentils on the Stove (40-45 min)

In a large pot (at least 3 quarts), combine $1/2$ cup of yellow lentils with 4 cups of water. Cook, uncovered, on medium heat for about 20 minutes, keeping an eye on it to make sure it does not overflow. (If you use a large pot and stir occasionally, this shouldn't happen.) After 20 minutes, when the water is no longer foaming and is largely soaked up by the lentils, add another 1 cup of water; reduce to medium heat and partially cover the pot. Cook for another 20-25 minutes. If the lentils dry out anytime during the cooking process, add another $1/2$ cup of water and keep cooking. Then, use a potato smasher or the back of a spoon to vigorously mash the lentils to break them up a bit, adding $1/4$ cup more of water if needed to achieve a smoother consistency.

The laziest Lentil?
Canned Lentils!

I'd be remiss not to mention canned lentils. Can you use them? Of course! Canned brown lentils will lend a stronger flavor, but if you're cool with that, you can easily swap in a full can of drained, unsalted lentils and skip the lentil-cooking bit entirely for the spinach dal, brown butter dal, tomato dal, and sambar recipes that follow.

Spinach Dal *in 25 minutes*

Ingredients

$^1/_2$ cup of red or yellow lentils
1   6-ounce bag of pre-washed spinach (or 5 ounces of frozen chopped spinach)
1   tablespoon of oil
$^1/_2$ teaspoon of crushed red pepper flakes
1   teaspoon of ground cumin powder
1   teaspoon of salt
2   tablespoons of lemon juice (bottled or fresh)
1   tablespoon of butter (optional)

Steps

1   Cook the lentils per the basic Lazy Lentil recipe of your choosing (see page 94). (I usually use Lazy Lentil Recipe #1 or #3 here.) While the lentils are cooking, move to step 2.

2   Roughly chop the spinach. Heat the oil in a large pan for 1 minute over medium-high heat. Add the red pepper flakes and cumin powder to the hot oil. After about 1 minute, add the spinach. Toss, cover, and cook for 4-5 minutes, or just until the spinach is wilted and bright green. Set aside.

3   Once the lentils have cooked, stir in the spinach, salt, lemon juice, and butter.

Serves 2-4.

Serve over rice or a toasted bagel or pita. You can also top with yogurt or raita.

Brown Butter & Spice Dal *in 25 minutes*

Ingredients

$^1/_2$ cup of red or yellow lentils
2   tablespoons of butter
1   teaspoon of black mustard seeds
1   teaspoon of cumin seeds
$^1/_2$ teaspoon of crushed red pepper flakes
1   teaspoon of turmeric powder
1   teaspoon of salt

Steps

1   Cook the lentils per the basic Lazy Lentil recipe of your choosing (see page 94). (I usually use Lazy Lentil Recipe #1 here.)

2   After the lentils have cooked, in a small pan, add the butter over medium heat. After about 2-3 minutes, or once the butter starts to brown, add the mustard and cumin seeds. Once one or two mustard seeds start popping, stir in the red pepper flakes and turmeric. After the spices have sizzled together for another 15-20 seconds, stir the butter, spices, and salt into the cooked lentils.

Serves 2-4.

Serve over warm pita or with rice.

Tip: For a quick meal, I like to eat these lentils over warm pita topped with salad greens and tomatoes.

Mango Dal *in 25 minutes*

Purists, like my dad, would say that mango dal must be made with raw green mango. But I've found that with the right combination of citrus juices and spices, you can create the perfect flavor with sweet mango, while cutting out that extra time of hunting down and cooking unripe fruit.

Ingredients

$^1/_2$ cup of red or yellow lentils
$1^1/_2$ cups of frozen mango chunks
$^1/_3$ cup of orange juice
1   tablespoon of oil
$^1/_2$ teaspoon of black mustard seeds
$^1/_2$ teaspoon of cumin seeds
$^3/_4$ teaspoon of red pepper powder
$^1/_4$ teaspoon of ground hing/asafoetida or ground ginger powder
1   teaspoon of salt
1   tablespoon of lemon juice (bottled or fresh)

Steps

1   Cook the lentils per the basic Lazy Lentil recipe of your choosing (see page 94), except add in the frozen mango chunks and orange juice in addition to the water that is called for in the recipe. (I use Lazy Lentil Recipe #1 here.) The lentils will be a bit goopy and not fully cooked.

2   Add the oil to a medium pot over medium heat, and after about 1 minute, add the mustard and cumin seeds. Once one or two mustard seeds start popping, stir in the red pepper powder and hing/ginger powder, and then add the cooked lentils and mango into the pot and thoroughly mix. Cook the lentils (uncovered) for about 8-10 minutes.

3   Once the lentils have cooked, stir in the salt and lemon juice.

Serves 2-4.

Goes well over rice with a drizzle of plain yogurt.

Tomato Dal _in 25 minutes_

Ingredients

$1/2$ cup of red or yellow lentils
1   tablespoon of oil
5-8 black peppercorns (optional)
$1/2$ teaspoon of black mustard seeds
$1/2$ teaspoon of cumin seeds
$1/2$ teaspoon of crushed red pepper flakes
$1/2$ teaspoon of turmeric powder
1   14.5-ounce can of diced tomatoes
1   teaspoon of salt
1   handful of cilantro (optional)

Steps

1   Cook the lentils per the basic Lazy Lentil recipe of your choosing (see page 94). (I like to use Lazy Lentil Recipe #1 here.) While the lentils are cooking, go to step 2.

2   Add the oil to a medium pot over medium heat. After about 1 minute, add the peppercorns (if using), mustard seeds, and cumin seeds to the oil. After one or two mustard seeds start popping, add the red pepper flakes and turmeric and cook for another 15 seconds before carefully pouring in the canned tomatoes and salt. Stir and cook (partially covered) for about 6-8 more minutes.

3   Once both the lentils and tomato sauce are ready, thoroughly combine them and cook together for 3-5 more minutes. If desired, roughly chop or tear the cilantro leaves and stir them in.

Serves 2-4.

Serve over rice, naan, or a whole wheat tortilla.

Tip: For more on how to infuse oil with spices, check out page 26.

Sambar *in 30 minutes*

I love making this traditional South Indian lentil soup, especially in the fall. This soup keeps for days, and it tastes even better the next day, after the flavors have had a chance to develop in the fridge—perfect for a warm lunch.

Ingredients

3/4	cup of red lentils
1	tablespoon of oil
1	onion
1	teaspoon of cumin seeds
1/2	teaspoon of black mustard seeds
2	cups of frozen yellow or butternut squash (or fresh yellow squash or pre-cut butternut squash)
1	14.5-ounce can of diced tomatoes
1	14.5-ounce can of diced potatoes (drained)
1	tablespoon of tamarind concentrate paste (found in natural/Indian food stores)
1	teaspoon of curry powder
1	teaspoon of garam masala powder
1	teaspoon of red pepper powder
1 1/2	teaspoons of salt
1	handful of cilantro (optional)

Steps

1   Combine the red lentils with 2 1/4 cups of water and otherwise cook per Lazy Lentil Recipe #1 (see page 94). While the lentils are cooking, move to step 2.

2   Add the oil to a large pot (an 8-quart size should work) over medium heat. Roughly chop the onion and the squash (as needed). Add the cumin and mustard seeds to the oil. Once one or two mustard seeds start popping, add in the onions and squash. Cover and cook for 8 minutes, stirring occasionally.

3   Once the lentils have cooked, add them along with all the remaining ingredients (except the cilantro) to the pot with the onions and squash. Stir in 2 cups of water. Thoroughly mix, cover, and cook on medium-high heat for 10 minutes. Roughly chop or tear the cilantro and stir it into the soup before serving.

Serves 4. Serve plain or over rice and drizzle with yogurt.

You won't find me baking gourds on any usual weeknight. But for a fancy fall dinner or Thanksgiving, I love to get butternut squash or small pumpkins, soften them in the microwave for two minutes, halve them, brush them with oil, and then bake them up while the sambar bubbles on the stove. It makes for a relatively easy, beautiful, and edible bowl.

Lemon Lentil Ginger Soup *in 25 minutes*

Ingredients

$^1/_2$ cup of red or yellow lentils
1   tablespoon of oil
8   black peppercorns
$^1/_2$ teaspoon of black mustard seeds
$^1/_4$ teaspoon of cumin seeds
$^1/_2$ teaspoon of red pepper flakes
$^1/_4$ teaspoon of turmeric powder
$^1/_2$ teaspoon of salt
$^1/_4$ teaspoon of curry powder
$^1/_8$ teaspoon of sugar (a pinch)
1   tablespoon of ginger paste (or fresh grated ginger)
3   tablespoons of bottled lemon juice (or the juice of one lemon)
1   handful of cilantro (optional)

Steps

1   Cook the lentils per the Lazy Lentil Recipe of your choice (see page 94). (I usually use Lazy Lentil Recipe #1 or #3 here.) While the lentils are cooking, go to step 2.

2   Add the oil to a medium pot over medium heat. After about 1 minute, add the peppercorns, mustard seeds, and cumin seeds. Once one or two mustard seeds start popping, add the red pepper flakes, and after about 15 seconds, carefully pour in 2 cups of water and mix in the turmeric, salt, curry powder, sugar, and ginger paste. Cover and boil this light broth until the lentils are cooked.

3   Add the lentils to the boiling broth. Cook together for about 5 more minutes. Remove from heat and then stir in the lemon juice. Roughly chop or tear the cilantro and stir it into the soup before serving.

Serves 2-4.

Tomato Rasam *in 25 minutes*

Ingredients

1	tablespoon of oil
$^1/_2$	teaspoon of cumin seeds
$^1/_2$	teaspoon of black mustard seeds
$^3/_4$	teaspoon of crushed red pepper flakes
1	14.5-ounce can of diced tomatoes
$^1/_2$	teaspoon of salt
1	teaspoon of tamarind concentrate paste (found in natural/Indian food stores)
$^1/_2$	teaspoon of turmeric powder
$^1/_2$	teaspoon of curry powder
$^1/_8$	teaspoon of sugar (just a pinch)
1	handful of cilantro

Steps

1   Add the oil to a medium pot over medium heat. After about 1 minute, add the cumin and mustard seeds. Once one or two mustard seeds start popping, add the red pepper flakes. After about 15 seconds, carefully stir in the remaining ingredients (except for the cilantro). Using a fork or potato smasher, lightly smash the tomatoes. Cook this sauce over medium-high without a cover for about 8 minutes.

2   When the sauce is the consistency of a thick marinara sauce and is just beginning to dry out, add 2 cups of water and stir. Partially cover and allow this soup to come to a boil. Then, uncover and boil for about 5 more minutes. Roughly chop or tear the cilantro and stir it into the soup before serving.

Serves 2.

Serve plain or over rice and top with a dollop of yogurt.

Spicy Lemon Rasam *in 10 minutes*

This intensely flavored broth reminds me of a spicy vegetarian version of chicken noodle soup—great for when you feel a cold coming on.

Ingredients

1	teaspoon of oil
$1/4$	teaspoon of fenugreek seeds
$1/2$	teaspoon of cumin seeds
$1/8$	teaspoon of ground clove (a pinch)
$1/4$	teaspoon of black mustard seeds
$1/4$	teaspoon of crushed red pepper flakes
$1/2$	teaspoon of salt
1	handful of cilantro
2	tablespoons of lemon juice (bottled or fresh)

Steps

1   Add the oil to a medium pot over medium heat. After about 30 seconds, add the first four spices. Once one or two mustard seeds start popping, add the red pepper flakes. After about 15 seconds, carefully add 3 cups of water and the salt. Cook, uncovered, and bring the broth to a boil.

2   Once the broth has been boiling for 3-5 minutes, remove from heat. Roughly chop or tear the cilantro, and add it and the lemon juice to the broth.

Serves 2-4.

This spicy broth is best served over plain rice.

Tip: For something fancier resembling a dumpling soup, try this broth over the Pongal Veggie Balls at page 118— they're not just for kids!

Pictured with Pongal Veggie Balls (see page 118).

Garlic Chickpea Soup *in 25 minutes*

Ingredients

1	tablespoon of oil
1	small onion
1	tablespoon of minced garlic (bottled or fresh)
$1/2$	teaspoon of ginger paste (or grated fresh ginger)
$1/2$	teaspoon of crushed red pepper flakes
1	15.5-ounce can of chickpeas/garbanzo beans
1	14.5-ounce can of diced potatoes
2	teaspoons of salt
$1/4$	teaspoon of turmeric powder
$1/4$	teaspoon of ground cumin
$1/4$	teaspoon of sugar
$1/8$	black pepper (a pinch)
1	tablespoon of butter or margarine (optional)

Steps

1   Add the oil to a medium pot over medium heat. Roughly chop the onion. Add the onion, garlic, ginger, and red pepper flakes to the oil. Toss, cover, and cook for about 5 minutes or until the onions begin to brown.

2   Drain the chickpeas and potatoes and add them to the onions. Cook everything together, uncovered, for 3-5 more minutes. Add 3 cups of water and the remaining ingredients, except the butter. Cover and bring to a boil. Then simmer for 5-8 minutes more.

3   Blend the soup to your desired texture. (An immersion blender works great here, but you can also use a regular blender with a vented lid to release steam.) Stir in the butter or margarine, if you like.

Serves 2-4.

Serve with toasted bread or croutons.

Lentils, Rice, and the Comforts of Home

We all have our comfort foods. Mine is rice with lentils. The aroma of rice and lentils cooking together always transports me back to my parents' living room. When I was a particularly picky six-year-old, my mom would take the rice and lentils that would invariably remain on my dinner plate, roll them into little balls, and feed them to me while I was distracted by the TV—the scent of recently minced chilies and garlic still lingering on her fingers. (Her fear that I would otherwise starve also led to a highly relaxed television protocol, which resulted in me watching "Moonlighting" way earlier than I should have.) Because it was what I ate at home as a kid, rice with lentils is now my comfort food. But ironically, this simple meal has its origins in a place that had once left me unsettled.

I was born and raised in Ohio. The little I knew of India and our extended family came from the rare letter or static-filled call, often relaying news of a birth or death of someone I didn't know. On occasion, India would send me a gift. A cardboard arrival whose battered exteriors hinted at a difficult journey around the world. I vividly remember a red dress, or "langa," that my relatives sent me when I was eight. The full-length dress came with its own slip and jacket and was covered in thick yellow and green embroidery which held in place hundreds of thumbnail-sized decorative mirrors. Every square inch of this dress was afflicted with thread and glass, and the jacket was not spared. In hindsight, I can see that though this dress was different, it was beautiful. But my first-generation, third-grade radar was on high alert for all antecedents of embarrassment. After all, I had just made it through Thanksgiving, when all the talk of Pilgrims and Indians somehow led my classmates to ridicule me about living in a teepee. Wrong on so many levels. Because this dress was a clear and present danger to my low-profile existence, it remained in the back of my closet. On occasion, my father would nostalgically pull out the dress and suggest that I wear it. I usually refused. Eventually, a growth spurt saved me. The dress was disassembled and stored away for safe keeping. I felt both relieved and guilty. And so it was with India.

Our lives were pretty much "Americanized," as my relatives liked to say. My parents didn't join Indian associations or celebrate Indian holidays, and I didn't speak a word of their native tongue. But one piece of that life remained strong: the food. Even before I learned to cook much else, I made rice with lentils. I made it a lot when I started living on my own. I guess something about the complete protein made me feel whole too.

Years later, I visited India for the first time. Over the course of two weeks, we met over forty relatives. As I caught glimpses of their lives, I was struck by how similar we were. My aunts and uncles were busy working long days at the office and raising their kids. My seven-year-old cousin was obsessed with "Krrish," the latest Indian action hero. I shared a strong resemblance to my teenage cousin-sisters, except that they seemed to possess the perfect balance of hipness and tradition. Their jeans, cell phones, and dancing abilities were light years ahead of my own, and I admired the way they glided between English and Telugu. I hadn't imagined these lives back when I received that red dress. But I was also peppered with questions ranging from the garden to slightly judgmental variety. How long do people date in America? Why didn't you ever learn traditional dancing? Don't you ever go to temple? Do you have any Indian friends? Some of these conversations rekindled a feeling of unease . . . of not quite belonging. Where were those third-grade defenses when I needed them?

Food became my saving grace. Dishes I had only seen on my mother's table were commonplace here, and the family seemed pleasantly surprised by my interest in Indian cuisine. We dined on hot tomato dal in my great uncle's house and bowls of lemon rice at my grandmother's place. My aunts eagerly showed off their spices and kitchen equipment. I admired their deep-frying spatulas and cleverly designed, multi-compartmented, stainless-steel spice boxes ("masala dabbas").

Just as we came, we left India in a whirlwind. We said goodbyes to what seemed like half the city. As we entered the airport, my Aunt Rukku ran up to me out of breath, extending a parting gift: a shiny masala dabba, with my name engraved on the lid. I gave her a big hug and squeezed the box into my suitcase. This was a gift I knew I would use.

After our trip, we resumed our lives. India called to make sure we arrived home safely. For a while, email traffic across the Pacific was regular. Then, life overtook our efforts to stay in close touch. Still, with only one trip, an absence which had been with me all my life was so much more palpable. One day, I received an email from Aunt Rukku. Her message was general: everyone wished us well; my grandmother was in good health; when would we come again? But as I scrolled down, she surprised me by sending her recipe for sweet Pongal (a rice and lentil dessert). I smiled and clicked *Print*. Okay, so maybe I would never be able to put on a sari in my sleep or fully appreciate the life-altering consequences of my horoscope. But India and I, we'd always have rice and lentils.

Pongal (Lentils with Rice) *in 15 minutes*

When I'm stretched to the max but want something healthy, this is my lazy lentil lunch. It's so warm and delicious that sometimes I eat it standing in the kitchen over my stove. This meal is a departure from traditional Indian "pongal," which typically uses split yellow mung dal and roasted cashews. I use red dal because it cooks faster! This meal is me at my laziest, but we all have those days, right?

Ingredients

$1/3$ cup of red lentils
$1/3$ cup of rice
1   tablespoon of butter or oil
5-8   black peppercorns (optional)
$1/2$ teaspoon of cumin seeds
$1/4$ teaspoon of turmeric powder
$1/2$ teaspoon of salt

Steps

1   Combine the lentils and rice with 2 cups of water in a large microwavable dish and microwave for about 15 minutes. While the lentils and rice are cooking, move to step 2.

2   In a small pan, add the butter or oil over medium heat. After about 1 minute, add the peppercorns. After about 30 seconds, add the remaining ingredients into the oil. Make sure the spices are coated with the oil so that the oil can be infused with their flavor. After another 30 seconds, remove the pan from the heat before the spices darken too much.

3   Once they are fully cooked, fluff the rice and lentils with a fork and stir in the butter and spices. (A rubber spatula works well for scraping the pan and getting all the spices out.)

Serves 2.

Serve plain or with yogurt or raita. I also like to eat this with spicy mango pickle— a condiment that you can get from any Indian grocery store.

Pongal Veggie Balls for Kids (and grownups) *in 20 minutes*

I rediscovered the utility of plain lentils and rice when my son started eating solid foods. You can add in a good dose of veggies into these bite-sized rice and lentil balls. These became a staple for us during the daycare years, when we needed to supplement the meat-heavy school lunches.

Ingredients

$^1/_2$	cup of red lentils
$^1/_2$	cup of rice
1	cup of frozen mixed vegetables
1	tablespoon of butter (optional)
$^1/_4$	teaspoon salt (optional)

Steps

1 Combine all the ingredients with 2 $^1/_2$ cups of water in a large microwavable dish and microwave for 15-17 minutes.

2 After the rice and lentil mixture is fully cooked, let it cool for a few minutes. Scoop out a heaping tablespoon of the rice and lentil mixture and use your hands to roll it into a ball. Make the desired number of Pongal balls and refrigerate the rest for later.

Serves 2.

GO-TO
GRAINS

As one of the world's top rice-consuming countries, it's no wonder that rice is to India as the baguette is to France and pasta is to Italy. In many parts of India, rice is eaten at every meal.

For vegetarians, rice is a key nutritional counterpart to lentils, combining to form a complete protein. Like other foods in India, many traditional rice dishes are cooked with a range of authentic (and time-consuming) ingredients, like soaked tamarind pulp or freshly grated coconut.

This chapter focuses on simplifying some of these traditional dishes with easy ingredients and techniques to speed up the cooking time, while maintaining a rich flavor.

Jeera Rice

Pea & Carrot Pilaf

Potato Spice Rice

Tomato Bath

Simple Curd Rice

Coconut & Peanut Rice

Lemon Rice

Pulihora

"Chicken" Biryani

Simple Upma

Wheat & Potatoes

Rava Dosa

Rice, Marriage, and Bridging the Gaps

Rice can often be an afterthought to a meal. And for some people, like my husband Mike, it's a dispensable part of any meal. Mike has never been too fond of white rice, but with his odd manner of eating it, it's easy to see why. When served Indian food, he eats each item separately, invariably treating the rice as some perfunctory dollop of dry mashed potatoes sitting next to a juicy steak. "Nobody eats their rice plain," I used to say in exasperation. How did he not know the "right" way of eating rice? You know, with equal portions of rice and curry in every spoonful, but never all pre-mixed on your plate—the very neurotic way I eat it, of course.

Our dispute came to a head when we attended a South Indian wedding and were each presented with a traditional thali platter: a food separatist's conundrum. The large steel plate arrived, draped with a bright green banana leaf, topped with eight small silver bowls of broths, spicy dals, and assorted vegetables—all encircling a large mound of white rice. The rice was meant to be eaten with each of the savory dishes, but Mike carried on his usual way, finishing each item before moving on to the next, and barely touching the plate's centerpiece.

After his rice was involuntarily topped off more than once, Mike subtly began tracking the rice-server around the room. (Yes, there was a waiter whose primary job was to make sure your rice mountain never diminished to a plateau.) But soon enough, Mike turned to speak with a relative when the mustached waiter appeared out of nowhere, holding an oversized pot of rice. Mike somehow found the courage to give a polite "no thank you." The server looked puzzled and started to reach forward anyway. Mike refused again, a little louder—this time hovering a protective hand over his half-eaten mound. Curious eyes began to peer in our direction. I nudged Mike under the table. We had already caused quite a stir earlier when someone noticed we were both left-handers, eating with the "wrong" hand. "But sir, this is white rice!" pleaded the server. Surely, this American must be confused. "No thank you," Mike said firmly, following up with one of the worst things you can possibly say in this setting, "I'm not hungry."

Stunned, the server walked away to consult with others. Guests came forward to press Mike—was something wrong with the food? Had he tried the bitter gourd sambar? Was he ill? When the commotion subsided, Mike slumped backed into his chair and murmured "I just don't understand how anyone can eat so much rice." "Shhh!" I responded, even though it did seem like there was an excessive amount of rice-eating going on that day.

We survived the dinner, and Mike survived an evening of me opining on whether his food-separatist ways might be symptomatic of semi-latent personality traits like rigidity and isolationism, which I of course thought deserved extensive discussion and dissection.

My pushiness aside . . . years later, I can finally say I get where Mike was coming from. Nobody eats plain old white rice. Not really, anyway. So, if you are as unenthused about plain white rice as my husband, or you just want to change it up, then the recipes in this chapter are for you.

Some of the milder dishes—like jeera rice, pilaf, and lemon rice—are just flavorful enough to eat separately but they also won't overwhelm when paired with lentils and curries. And, if you are truly a separatist about the items on your plate, there are a few rice dishes here that are meals unto themselves—like biryani, tomato bath, and pulihora.

My small hope is that these recipes bring out the best in rice, so that it can really be a centerpiece of your meal. And, if we can help bridge the gap between the mixers, stackers, and purists among us—at the table if nowhere else—well, that's great too.

A fast-food version of a South Indian thali (served sans heaping mound of rice).

Almost-Minute Rice: The Basics

Unless you're using one of those brands of instant rice (and even then), it's going to take you more than a minute to make a rice dish. But with a little pre-planning, you can actually be quite efficient when cooking rice.

Generally, the first thing I do when I walk into my kitchen is start the rice. That way, it's always done by the time the rest of my meal is ready. Most of the dishes in this chapter require a fixed amount of "hands-off" cooking time, so that leaves you with a nice block of time to make something else.

There are many varieties of rice; unless I note otherwise, I recommend starting with white rice. Brown rice would be healthier and could work well in some of these recipes, but it takes a little longer to cook and it's not common in Indian cuisine, so just be mindful of that if you venture there.

There are also a few different ways to cook rice. Just as with lentils, you can use a pressure cooker or a rice cooker. You can also cook rice on the stove or in the microwave (my favorite weeknight method), so no special equipment is necessary. Here are some basic techniques for cooking white rice, which will serve as a foundation for the rice recipes in this book. (The recipes in this chapter were timed assuming the use of the microwave method, but you can use whatever cooking technique you prefer!)

Basic Quick Rice Techniques

Rice in the Microwave (15 min)

In a large glass microwavable bowl (at least 2.5 quarts), combine 1 cup of basmati, jasmine, or other white rice with 2 cups of water (i.e., 1 part rice to 2 parts water). Cook for about 15 minutes in the microwave, uncovered. Ideally, you will not need to stir or add any water while the rice is cooking. Afterwards, carefully remove the bowl from the microwave and fluff it with a fork. Add butter, oil, or ghee if you like. Note: if the rice is too hard after you remove it from the microwave, stir in $\frac{1}{4}$ cup of water and cook for 5 more minutes.

Rice on the Stove (20 min)

In a medium pot (about 3 quarts), combine 1 cup of basmati, jasmine, or other long grain white rice with 2 cups of water (i.e., 1 part rice to 2 parts water). Cook on medium heat, covered, for 15-20 minutes. Ideally, you will not need to stir or add any additional water while the rice is cooking but keep an eye on it to make sure it doesn't spill over or burn as it cooks. If it starts to spill over, keep the pot partially uncovered. Afterwards, fluff with a fork and add butter, oil, or ghee if you like.

Rice in the Pressure Cooker (10 min)

Follow the directions for your particular electric pressure cooker, but I generally use 1 cup of rice and 1 cup of water and use the manual/pressure cooking setting on the instant pot (this should take about 10 minutes).

Jeera Rice (Cumin Rice) *in 15 minutes*

This simple rice goes with any curry or lentil dish. It's just a slight step up from plain old white rice, but it's enough to elevate your meal from regular to restaurant quality.

Ingredients

1   cup of white rice
2   tablespoons of butter
1   heaping teaspoon of cumin seeds
$^1/_2$ teaspoon of salt

Steps

1   Cook the rice using the Basic Quick Rice technique of your choosing (see page 125). While the rice is cooking, move to step 2.

2   In a small pan over low-medium heat, heat the butter for 4-5 minutes. The butter should turn brown and start to foam. Remove the foam with a spoon. (This is a busy girl's ghee—you can also strain and discard the foamy milk solids, so you are left with just the clarified butter, but skimming off the foam with a spoon is just fine for this recipe!) Add the cumin seeds to the hot brown butter and toast for about 1 minute, removing the pan from the heat before the cumin seeds blacken. Set aside.

3   Once the rice is cooked, combine it with the cumin seeds and butter, and add the salt. (A rubber spatula works well to get all the butter from the pan.) Mix the rice well with two forks until the rice is evenly coated.

Serves 2-4.

Pea & Carrot Pilaf *in 20 minutes*

Traditionally, pilaf is made by toasting up raw rice grains in oil, spices, and sautéed vegetables, all before the rice even gets boiled. But if you're busy, you can basically get there by plopping everything in the microwave. Here's how . . .

Ingredients

10	baby carrots (or 2-3 medium carrots)
1	cup of white rice
1	cup of frozen green peas
$1/2$	teaspoon curry powder
$1/2$	teaspoon of garam masala powder
$1/4$	teaspoon of crushed red pepper flakes
$1/2$	teaspoon of salt
$1/8$	teaspoon of sugar (a pinch)
1	tablespoon of oil

Steps

1   Cut the baby carrots into slivers.

2   Stir all the ingredients together with 2 cups of water and cook the rice pilaf using the Basic Quick Rice technique of your choosing (see page 125). I love cooking this pilaf in the microwave—super easy.

3   When the rice is cooked, mix and fluff well with two forks.

Serves 2-4.

This is a fairly mild dish that is best served with curry, chutney, or lentils.

Tip: Switch things up by adding your favorite frozen veggies in place of the carrots and peas.

Potato Spice Rice *in 35 minutes*

This dish features a dry roasting technique that unlocks flavors and aromas of seeded spices that you can't draw out any other way. Full disclosure: there are a few moving parts that make this recipe a bit more complicated, so be sure to read ahead before you dive in. You'll end up with a crowd-pleaser that is well worth the teeny bit of extra effort.

Ingredients

4	small red-skinned potatoes
2	tablespoon of chana dal (dried split chick peas, found in natural/Indian food stores)
1	tablespoon of coriander seeds
1	teaspoon cumin seeds
$1/2$	teaspoon crushed red pepper flakes
$1/8$	teaspoon of clove powder (a pinch)
1	cup of white rice
1	tablespoon of oil
1	small onion
1	tablespoon of ketchup (or tomato sauce)
1	teaspoon of salt
1	handful of fresh cilantro (optional)

Steps

1   Wrap the potatoes in wet paper towels and microwave them for 4-5 minutes (we'll be roasting them as well, so you don't want them overcooked here). Meanwhile, move to step 2.

2   Dry roast the spices: add the chana dal, coriander, and cumin seeds to a large pan over medium heat. Dry roast for 2-3 minutes. Remove from heat and grind these spices along with the red pepper flakes and clove powder in a blender or spice grinder until you get a rough powder. Set aside and move to step 3.

3   Remove the potatoes from the microwave and then start cooking the rice using the Basic Quick Rice technique of your choosing (see page 125). Meanwhile, move to step 4.

4   Roughly chop the onion and cooked potatoes. Over medium heat, add the oil to the same (but empty) pan in which you roasted the spices. After 1 minute, add the onions and potatoes and fry them until lightly browned.

5 Combine the cooked rice, roasted spices, onions, potatoes, as well as the ketchup and salt. Fluff with a fork. If desired, roughly chop or tear the cilantro and garnish the rice.

Serves 2-4.

Potato spice rice with sambar.

Tomato Bath (Tomato Rice) *in 25 minutes*

If you're craving a one-pot comfort meal, tomato bath has the perfect combination of heartiness and zest.

Ingredients

1	cup of white rice
1	onion
1	tablespoon of oil
$1/4$	teaspoon of coriander seeds
$1/2$	teaspoon of black mustard seeds
$1/4$	teaspoon of crushed red pepper flakes
1	14.5-ounce can of diced tomatoes
$1/2$	teaspoon of turmeric powder
1	teaspoon of curry powder
$1/8$	teaspoon of clove powder (a pinch)
1	teaspoon of salt

Steps

1   Cook the rice using the Basic Quick Rice technique of your choosing (see page 125). While the rice is cooking, move to steps 2 and 3.

2   Chop the onion. Heat the oil in a medium pot over medium heat for about 1 minute. Add the coriander and mustard seeds to the oil and heat until one or two of the mustard seeds start popping. Stir in the onion and red pepper flakes. Cover and cook the onion until it becomes tender (about 3-5 minutes), stirring occasionally.

3   Once the onion is tender, stir in the tomatoes, turmeric, curry powder, clove powder, and salt; cover. Let the tomato sauce simmer over low heat for about 5 minutes. Slightly mash the tomatoes with a fork or potato smasher.

4   Once the rice is cooked, fluff it with a fork and then stir or swirl in the warm tomato sauce until it is mixed to your liking.

Serves 2-4.

Tomato bath can be served as a stand-alone meal, or with plain lentils and yogurt.

Simple Curd Rice *in 20 minutes*

Curd rice is a mild and creamy dish with just the right crunchy kick. Some say that it helps with digestion, so it is often eaten at the end of the meal. It's a comfort food for me and I always have it with spicy mango pickle—a condiment that you can buy from any local or online Indian grocery store.

Ingredients

1   cup of white rice
1   tablespoon of oil
$1/2$ teaspoon of black mustard seeds
$1/4$ teaspoon of crushed red pepper flakes
$1/8$ teaspoon of ground hing/asafoetida powder or ginger powder (a pinch)
1   cup of plain yogurt
$1/4$ teaspoon of salt

Steps

1   Cook the rice using the Basic Quick Rice technique of your choosing (see page 125).

2   Heat the oil in a small pan or pot over medium heat. After about one minute, add the mustard seeds. Once one or two mustard seeds start popping, stir in the crushed red pepper flakes and asafoetida/ginger. Cook for about 15-30 seconds so that the oil is infused but the spices do not burn; remove the pan from the heat.

3   Combine $1\,1/2$ cups of the cooked rice, the oil and spices, the yogurt, the salt, and $1/4$ cup of water. (Reserve the remainder of the rice as leftovers.) Stir the yogurt rice well with a fork. (Add more yogurt if you prefer a saucier consistency and less for a firmer consistency.)

Serves 2-4.

Serve immediately. Curd rice goes well with spicier dishes or can be eaten plain.

Curd rice with spicy mango pickle.

Making Friends and Fast Flavors

As I search for faster ways to cook the food I love, I'm sometimes reminded of why I love to cook. Besides the ultimate reward of eating, the process of cooking can reconnect you to life—sometimes rekindling memories of friends, loved ones, and the way we were. This occurred to me as I was thinking of techniques for quickly flavoring rice dishes, and I had a flashback to when I was a kid, watching the mother of a Japanese friend prepare rice.

I met my friend Natsuyo in elementary school in Columbus, Ohio. While welcoming in many ways, our school did not always know how to handle the influx of cultural diversity that came with being in a large college town. To start with, they put me in an English-as-a-Second Language class—even though I was born in America, English was my first and only language, and I was doing just fine in reading and writing. I was also consistently assigned to be the "classroom partner" for any new kid at school with a foreign background. And then there was the time I got to be Mrs. Claus in the school's big Christmas play and a teacher painted white makeup all over my face right before I went onstage. In the end, despite these practices (or maybe because of some of them), I got so much more exposure to different cultures and cuisines. I ended up with great friends with faces of all shades.

So that's how I met Natsuyo from Japan. She was only at our school for a year or so, but as I was her assigned class partner, we became fast friends. I was also introduced to Japanese food at her home. I'll admit that my first brush with raw tofu probably put me off soy-based products for a good decade. But when her mom made ochazuke—a soupy rice with green tea and vegetables—I felt warm and cozy. When she tilted her cast iron kettle over our bowls of rice, the steamy golden sea that hugged the grains made even the unfamiliar flavors of nori and wasabi feel welcoming.

In the years that followed, my classroom assignments led me to meet Tim from the Philippines, Aisha from Nigeria, and Fang from China. I absorbed a variety of details, small and large from my friends, usually over meals in their homes or mine. I learned that some people eat watermelon mixed with rice. I learned that the housing projects next to our school were not mysterious; they were just where some of my friends lived. And I learned that sometimes we're different, but more often than not we're just coming to each other from different places.

Years later, pondering over pearls of grain in my own kitchen, I remembered devouring that green-tea infused rice. Although I've learned that rice is pre-cooked in ochazuke, that concept of steeping rice in a flavorful broth or juice (instead of just water) seemed like it could be an efficient way of directly flavoring the absorbent grain. So, I've tried to incorporate this idea of quick infusion in many of my recipes.

To be sure, there was some trial and error—the success of this technique depends on the viscosity of your cooking liquid, as well as its flavor. Sadly, lemonade-rice didn't make the cut. But infusion has worked well for making dishes like coconut peanut rice (where rice is cooked directly in coconut water), lemon rice (where rice is cooked in lemon juice), and even some lentil dishes like mango dal, where lentils are cooked in orange juice! When I make these dishes, I am reminded of the meals I had at Natsuyo's house. But more than that, I'm reminded of all those friends who infused my childhood with interesting experiences, large and small.

Coconut & Peanut Rice *in 20 minutes*

The flavor of this coconut-infused rice combined with crunchy peanuts is unique and yet easy to create. I first made it in an effort to finish off a jumbo can of honey roasted peanuts that I had left over from a party. Peanuts aren't my favorite thing, but now I even save those little airplane packets in anticipation of making this dish.

Ingredients

1	cup of white rice
2	cups of coconut water (canned or bottled)
1	tablespoon of oil
1	teaspoon of cumin seeds
1	teaspoon of black mustard seeds
$1/2$	teaspoon of red pepper powder
$1/2$	cup of peanuts (plain, salted, or honey roasted is fine)
2	tablespoons of sweetened or unsweetened coconut flakes (optional)
1	teaspoon of salt

Steps

1   Cook the rice using the Basic Quick Rice technique of your choosing (see page 125), except instead of cooking the rice in water, cook the rice in an equivalent amount of coconut water. As the rice cooks, move to step 2.

2   Heat the oil in a large pot or deep pan over medium heat. (The pan should be large enough to hold and toss 3 cups of cooked rice.) After about 45 seconds, add the cumin and mustard seeds. Once one or two mustard seeds start popping, stir in the red pepper powder and peanuts. (And if you're using coconut flakes, add them to the pan here too and lightly toast them up.) Let the peanuts and spices fry together for about 1 minute, then turn off the heat.

3   When the rice is cooked, add it and the salt to your pot of peanuts and spices. Using two forks, toss the rice, salt, and peanut and spice mixture, and cook over medium heat for 2 more minutes. (Add 1-4 tablespoons of water if the rice is too dry or starts to burn.)

Serves 2-4.

Lemon Rice *in 20 minutes*

Ingredients

1	cup of white rice
$1/3$	cup of lemon juice (bottled or fresh)
1	tablespoon of oil
1	teaspoon of black mustard seeds
$1/8$	teaspoon of fenugreek seeds (optional)
$1/4$	teaspoon of crushed red pepper flakes
$1/4$	teaspoon of turmeric powder
1	teaspoon of salt
$1/2$	teaspoon of sugar

Steps

1   Cook the rice using the microwave or stovetop Basic Quick Rice technique (see page 125), except instead of cooking the rice in 2 cups of water, use 1 $2/3$ cups of water and $1/3$ cup of lemon juice. While the rice is cooking, move to step 2.

2   Add the oil to a small pan over low-medium heat. After about 1 minute, add the mustard and fenugreek seeds (if using) to the hot oil. Once one or two mustard seeds start popping, add the red pepper flakes and turmeric powder and heat for 30 seconds more. Then remove the pan from the heat and set it aside.

3   Once the rice is cooked, add the oil and spices to the rice (a rubber spatula works well to get all the spices out of the pan). Sprinkle in the salt and sugar. Mix well with two forks until the rice is evenly coated.

Serves 2-4.

Pulihora (Tamarind Rice) *in 25 minutes*

This tangy rice with fruit and nuts is one of my favorites. It's popular among the temple scenes in South India, but I like it any old time. Pulihora is traditionally made by soaking and straining tamarind fruit pods into a paste, which gives this rice its trademark flavor. We'll use a tamarind concentrate paste here and cook the rice directly in it to achieve the same rich flavor in much less time.

Ingredients

1	cup of white rice
1¹/₂	tablespoons of tamarind concentrate paste (found in natural/Indian food stores)
1	tablespoon oil
¹/₂	teaspoon of black mustard seeds
¹/₂	teaspoon of cumin seeds
¹/₄	cup of peanuts (plain, salted, or honey roasted is fine)
¹/₄	cup of raisins
¹/₄	teaspoon red pepper powder
1	teaspoon turmeric powder
1	teaspoon of salt
¹/₂	teaspoon sugar

Steps

1   Cook the rice using the Basic Quick Rice technique of your choosing (see page 125), except add in ¹/₄ cup more of water and stir in the tamarind concentrate paste into the water before cooking. Stir the rice periodically while it cooks and move to step 2.

2   Add the oil to a small pan over medium heat. After about 1 minute, add the mustard and cumin seeds and cook until one or two mustard seeds start popping; add the peanuts and raisins; toss and cook for about 1 more minute. When the raisins plump up, stir in the red pepper powder, turmeric, salt, and sugar, along with ¹/₄ cup of water. Simmer together for another minute and then remove from heat.

3   As soon as the rice is cooked, combine it and the peanut-raisin-spice sauce into your serving dish. (A rubber spatula works well to get all the spices and oil out of your pan.) Mix well with two forks until the rice is evenly coated.

Serves 2-4.

"Chicken" Biryani *in 30 minutes*

Classic chicken biryani can be time consuming because the rice is often cooked in stages and layered with many spices and sauces, not to mention that a whole chicken must be prepped, marinated, and cooked! This recipe substitutes in faux chicken and compresses the layers into three: cooked potatoes, aromatic rice, and a tangy "chicken" sauce. There are a lot of spices here, but don't let the list fool you— the work is minimal, and you can make this meal in about half an hour.

Ingredients

3-4	small red-skinned potatoes
1	cup of frozen meatless "chicken" strips (*e.g.*, meatless chicken strips from Morningstar Farms or Beyond Meat)
1	large onion
1	cup of basmati rice
1	tablespoon of curry powder
$1/4$	teaspoon of red pepper powder
$3/4$	teaspoon of ground cardamom
$1/4$	teaspoon of clove powder
$1/2$	teaspoon of ground cinnamon
$1/4$	teaspoon of turmeric powder
2	tablespoons of raisins
2	teaspoons of salt (total)
3	tablespoons of oil (total)
2	tablespoons of minced garlic (bottled or fresh)
1	teaspoon of ginger paste (or powder)
$1/2$	cup of plain yogurt
$1/4$	cup of tomato paste

Steps

1 Wrap the potatoes in wet paper towels and microwave them for 4-5 minutes (we'll be roasting them later, so you don't want them overcooked here). Meanwhile, remove the meatless chicken from the freezer and thinly slice the onion. After the potatoes have cooked, remove them from the microwave and set aside.

2 In a microwavable bowl, combine the rice with the next 7 listed ingredients (curry, red pepper, cardamom, clove, cinnamon, turmeric, and raisins), and 1 teaspoon of the salt and 1 teaspoon of oil. Add water and cook per the Basic Quick Rice technique of your choosing (see page 125). (If using the microwave, stir the rice about halfway through and add a few more tablespoons of water if the rice dries out.) While the rice cooks, move to step 3.

3   In a large pan, heat 2 tablespoons of oil over medium heat. Cut the meatless
    chicken and cooked potatoes into chunks. Add the garlic, ginger, sliced onion,
    and 1 teaspoon of salt to one side of the pan. Add the potatoes and chicken to
    the other, and allow them all to lightly brown, stirring minimally to develop a
    crunchy coating on the potatoes. Roast for 5-6 minutes. Then, stir in the
    yogurt and tomato paste and cook everything for 2-3 more minutes.

4   Once the rice is cooked, toss it together with the potato-onion-chicken sauce.
    Drizzle the rice with the remaining oil, if desired.

Serves 2-4. Serve plain or with yogurt and fresh mint.

Simple Upma *in 15 minutes*

In India, this mildly spiced wheat dish is usually eaten for breakfast, but it works well any time of the day as a quick hearty snack or light meal that you can make with minimal ingredients and effort.

Ingredients

1	small onion
1	tablespoon of butter or oil
$1/2$	teaspoon of cumin seeds
$1/4$	teaspoon of crushed red pepper flakes
$1/2$	teaspoon of salt
1	tablespoon of vinegar (any kind)
$3/4$	cup of frozen mixed vegetables (optional)
$1/2$	cup of wheat farina cereal (cream of wheat)

Steps

1 Chop the onion. Add the butter or oil to a medium pot over low-medium heat and after about 30 seconds, add the cumin seeds, red pepper flakes, and the onion. Once the onions become translucent, add 1 cup of water along with the salt, vinegar, and frozen veggies, if using. Stir and cover this broth and cook on medium-high heat.

2 After the broth and veggies have cooked for 5-6 minutes and the broth is boiling, slowly pour in the cream of wheat, while continuously stirring. When the cream of wheat is thoroughly combined and there are no lumps, cover and cook for about 1 more minute and then remove the pot from the heat.

Serves 2-4.

Eat warm and top with yogurt, if desired. Or turn this into an easy finger food by pressing the cooked upma into a small square container. Once cooled, invert the container, and carefully slice the upma-cube into squares.

Wheat & Potatoes *in 20 minutes*

Whoever said that the potato's perfect partner was meat? This dish resembles polenta and risotto, except that it's much easier to make!

Ingredients

1	onion
1	tablespoon of oil
$1/2$	teaspoon of black mustard seeds
$1/2$	teaspoon of cumin seeds
1	teaspoon of salt
$1/8$	teaspoon of clove powder (a pinch)
$1/4$	teaspoon of red pepper powder
$1/2$	teaspoon of ginger paste or powder
1	14.5-ounce can of diced potatoes (drained)
1	14.5-ounce can of diced tomatoes or 1 cup of fresh cherry tomatoes
1	handful of fresh cilantro (optional)
$1/2$	cup of wheat farina cereal (cream of wheat)

Steps

1   Roughly chop the onion. In a medium pot, heat the oil over medium heat for 30 seconds and then add the mustard and cumin seeds. Once one or two mustard seeds start popping, stir in the onion. Once the onions are translucent, add 1 $1/2$ cups of water and the next five listed ingredients (salt, clove, red pepper, ginger, and drained potatoes). If you are using canned tomatoes, add them here as well (but hold off on fresh tomatoes). Stir and cover. While you are cooking this broth, move to step 2.

2   Roughly chop the cilantro and if you are using cherry tomatoes, cut the tomatoes in half.

3   Once the broth comes to a boil, slowly pour in the cream of wheat and stir continuously. When all the cream of wheat is evenly combined with the water and spices, add in the cilantro and the cherry tomatoes (if using). Fluff with a fork and cover and cook for about 2-3 more minutes.

Serves 2-4.

Rava Dosas *in 20 minutes*

Traditionally, an Indian "dosa" is a crepe made from a batter of lentils and rice which are soaked, blended, and then fermented overnight—all before the frying process has even begun. This is a quicker version called a "rava dosa." It's faster because it uses farina and lemon in lieu of the whole fermented-lentil-batter thing. It's a little different, but for my taste and schedule, I don't miss the lentil-version, and I don't think you will either!

Ingredients

- $1/2$ cup of all-purpose flour
- $1/2$ cup of white rice flour
- $1/2$ cup of plain yogurt
- $1/4$ cup of wheat farina cereal/cream of wheat (you can also use rava-semolina flour)
- $1/2$ teaspoon of salt
- $1/4$ teaspoon of crushed red pepper flakes
- $1/4$ teaspoon of cumin seeds
- 2 tablespoons of lemon juice (fresh or bottled)
- 3-5 tablespoons of oil for frying (total)

Steps

1   In a large bowl, thoroughly mix all the ingredients (except the oil) with $1 1/2$ cups of water. This is your dosa batter. (The batter should have a consistency that is between pancake and crepe batter.)

2   Over medium to high heat, spread 1 teaspoon of oil in large nonstick frying pan (at least 10") and heat the oil for about 1 minute (you can also use cooking spray). Pour about $1/2$ a cup of the batter in the pan. Using the back of a spoon, quickly spread the batter so that it resembles a thin pancake or crepe. Allow the dosa to fry for about 1-2 minutes. Once the bottom is a dark golden brown, flip the dosa over and cook the other side. (Just like with pancakes, the bottom will not brown the same way the top does but when the batter no longer oozes out, the dosa is cooked—about 1-2 minutes on each side.)

3   Repeat the process for the remaining batter.

Serves 2-4.

These are best eaten hot off the stove. Dosas are often served with yellow potato and mustard seed curry (page 88). You can also just eat them plain, with ketchup or butter, or with yogurt and spicy mango pickle.

Tip: Change things up by adding minced onions and cilantro to your dosa batter!

DESSERTS IN A DASH

When I was a little girl, Indian sweets just couldn't keep up with chocolate candy bars. But as my taste buds matured and my teeth became sufficiently candied up by high fructose corn syrup, I've begun to crave the rich rice puddings and creamy milk-based sweets that are the hallmarks of Indian desserts. Just because you're pressed for time doesn't mean your sweet cravings go away. And with a few tasteful shortcuts and some key ingredients, you can have dessert covered for a couple of nights, no problem.

Mysore Pak

Coconut Burfi Bites

Rava Ladu Cookies

Gulabjamuns

Rasmalai

Coconut Rice Pudding

Carrot Halwa Pudding

Kesari

Sweet Pongal

Easy Indian Porridge

Fruit Lassi

Sweet Cardamom Nut Milk

Coconut Rummers

Mango Creamsicle

Indian Desserts: Delicious but Delayed

Indian desserts have a special warmth and soulful quality that you just won't find elsewhere. Unlike most American desserts, Indian sweets are often milk-based. During one of my trips to India, my aunt took me to a wonderful dessert shop. The aroma of warm milk, melted butter, and sugar filled the store, and the range of colorful cubes and cake-like balls was a visual feast. I returned several times during my short stay.

Some Indian desserts like rasmalai and rasgulas require curdling boiled milk and compressing out the whey using a cheesecloth to make a fresh milk "chenna" or sweet cheese. Other desserts like gulabjamuns and burfis begin with a painstaking stovetop reduction of whole milk to make "khoa" or milk fudge—a process that can be very time-consuming. While still others involve slow-cooking, grinding, soaking, and even getting sugary syrups to reach that crucial "soft-ball" candy-making stage. And once you get past all of that, many of the traditional recipes require special ingredients, like ghee, rose water, and jaggery.

Gulabjamuns made easy with pancake mix and milk powder.

I get discouraged just thinking about it, and I suspect that's why pre-packaged Indian desserts and mixes are so popular in Indian grocery stores. As much as I appreciate the hours that must go into these store-bought treats, I'm not going to replicate that process at home. Instead, I aim to use a variety of simple ingredients and timesaving techniques to recapture my favorite flavors.

Sweetened condensed milk, fast-cooking cream of wheat, and skipping some unnecessary measures are just a few ways that most of this chapter's recipes can be pulled off in 30 minutes or less.

We'll start with my shortcuts to five classic desserts: mysore pak, coconut burfi, rava ladus, gulabjamuns, and rasmalai. Once you get the hang of these recipes, you can experiment with new flavors by adding chocolate, nuts, and dried fruits. Then, we'll move to quick porridges and puddings, and I'll leave you with a few 5-minute drinks. I hope you enjoy the unique take on these exotic treats and the time saved.

Quick coconut burfi bites dipped in chocolate and topped with almonds.

Mysore Pak *in 25 minutes*

The closest comparison might be shortbread, but mysore pak is really unlike any other dessert. Traditionally, it is made with "ghee" or clarified butter, but plain old butter works for me. Mysore Pak is packed with protein, which I like to think makes up for all the sugar and butter!

Ingredients

1   cup of butter
2   cups of garbanzo bean/chickpea flour (found in natural/Indian food stores)
$1^1/_2$ cups of sugar (you can kick it up to $1^3/_4$ cups if you have a sweet tooth)
$^1/_4$ teaspoon of salt
1   teaspoon of vanilla

Steps

1   Over medium heat, melt the butter in a medium pot. Meanwhile, line a small 8-inch square pan or dish with wax paper.

2   Once the butter is completely melted and foaming (about 2-3 minutes), add in the rest of the ingredients and stir until the mixture is smooth like caramel. Cook and stir continuously. Remove from heat after about 4-5 minutes. (The mixture should be bubbling and pulling away from the sides of the dish when stirred.)

3   Immediately pour the hot mixture into your lined pan. Using a spoon or rubber spatula, spread the mixture evenly so that the surface is smooth. Allow the mysore pak to cool for 15 minutes or more in the refrigerator. Once this confectionery has set, carefully cut it into diamonds or squares. (It may help to first run your knife around the edges of the pan, invert the pan over a cutting board, and peel back the wax paper.)

Serves several.

Store the mysore pak candy in an airtight container. It usually tastes even better the second day!

Tip: For a special twist, stir in chocolate chips, chopped nuts, or popped popcorn, before you cool this in the fridge!

Coconut Burfi Bites *in 20 minutes*

This twist on a traditional South Indian dessert is a great way to introduce anyone to the region's unique sweet flavors. Forming little burfi balls is not only an exercise in cuteness and portion control, but it also eliminates the time that burfi normally takes to cook and set up, so you get a bite sooner!

Ingredients

2	cups of sweetened shredded coconut
1	cup of sweetened condensed milk

Steps

1   Preheat the oven to 350°F. In a bowl, thoroughly stir together the coconut and condensed milk. Spread the mixture thinly across an ungreased cookie sheet (lined with parchment paper, if cleanup is not your thing). The mixture does not have to cover the entire cookie sheet, just spread it as thinly as possible. Bake for 10 minutes. (The edges of the coconut mixture will brown, it's okay.)

2   Remove the coconut mixture from the oven and allow it to cool for about 5 minutes. Then, using your hands, form the somewhat sticky mixture into little tablespoon-sized balls. You should get about 16-20 balls. Cool the burfi balls in an airtight container in the fridge until you're ready to serve. (They'll firm up a bit more in the fridge.)

Serves several.

For a sophisticated presentation, serve the burfi bites in mini paper cupcake liners, like little truffles.

Tip: For fun variations, dip the finished coconut balls in melted chocolate, sprinkles, or roll the balls in chopped nuts or crushed freeze-dried strawberries.

Rava Ladu Cookies *in 20 minutes*

Ingredients

2	tablespoons of butter
1/4	cup of raisins
1	cup of wheat farina cereal (cream of wheat)
1/2	cup of sugar
1/3	cup of milk

Steps

1 Heat the butter in a medium pan over medium heat. Once the butter is melted, stir in the raisins and cook for 1-2 minutes or until the raisins plump up.

2 Add the cream of wheat to the butter. Stir and roast for 2-3 minutes or until the cream of wheat begins to turn a very pale golden color, then stir in the sugar. Cook and continually stir the mixture for 1-2 minutes, without letting the cream of wheat burn. Slowly add the milk, moistening all the cream of wheat. The mixture should resemble hot caramel and bubble for 1-2 more minutes (the longer you cook it, the harder and crunchier the ladus will be). Cool for 5 minutes.

3 While the mixture is still malleable, spoon out tablespoon-sized mounds and drop them onto wax paper or a plate—a cookie scooper works well, if you have one. (If the mixture remains too thin to scoop, cook it for another minute or so; if the mixture is too crumbly, stir in a little cold milk.) The cookies will harden slightly. You should get about 15 cookies.

Serves several.

Store in an airtight container.

Tip: Swap in your choice of dried fruit or nuts for a different twist. Chocolate chips can also be added after the mixture has cooled.

Gulabjamuns *in 35 minutes*

Gulabjamuns are traditionally made with "khoa"—a thick milk paste that is made by slowly stirring hot milk for hours. We save time by using dry milk powder and pancake mix instead. After that first bite into this warm pudding-like cake, it'll be hard to eat just one.

Ingredients

1$\frac{1}{3}$	cups of sugar
$\frac{1}{2}$	teaspoon of ground cardamom
6-8	cups of vegetable oil (or enough for deep frying)
1	cup of instant nonfat dry milk powder
1	cup of complete pancake mix
$\frac{1}{3}$	cup of milk
2	tablespoons of softened butter

Steps

1 Whisk the sugar, cardamom, and 2 cups of water in a medium pot over medium heat. Allow this sugar-water to come to a gentle boil, uncovered, while you move to the next steps. (The goal here is a thin simple syrup.)

2 In a large pot over medium heat on the back burner, add about 6 cups of oil for deep frying. (Or use a deep fryer if you prefer.) The exact amount of oil will depend on the size of your pot, but you basically want enough oil so that your gulabjamuns will be fully immersed while frying, but the pot should be no more than half full. Allow the oil to slowly heat as you move to step 3. (You want the oil to stay right under 350°F.)

3 While the oil is heating, combine the milk powder, pancake mix, milk, and butter with your hands to form a dough (don't knead it). The dough should be very soft and a bit sticky. Use your hands to form the dough into tablespoon-sized balls. (Try making the balls as smooth as possible; deep cracks will cause the dough to fall apart while frying.) Cover completed balls with a wet paper towel as you go.

4 Test the oil's temperature by dropping in a small piece of dough; it should begin to sizzle slowly, but not brown immediately (between 325°-350°F). When the oil is ready, carefully place the balls in the oil using a long, slotted metal spoon to prevent splatter. Fry the balls for about 3-4 minutes, rotating frequently until golden brown. Remove each of the fried balls and place them into the hot sugar syrup; remove from heat.

Serves several.

Store the gulabjamuns in the simple syrup in the fridge. You can serve them after a few minutes of soaking (less sweet) or allow them to soak longer (sweeter).

Tip: When forming the balls, if the mixture is too crumbly, add more milk, a tablespoon at a time, until you get the right consistency. If it's too sticky, add a bit more pancake mix, a tablespoon at a time.

Rasmalai *in 50 minutes (mostly inactive baking time)*

Traditional rasmalai is made by boiling milk, forming milk curds into little cakes, and then soaking the cakes in a milk sauce that's flavored with blanched nuts and spices. Some use ricotta cheese as an easy shortcut, but this recipe goes even further by using ice cream to instantly capture the essence of the perfect sauce. A shameless secret, I know, but once you try it, you may never go back.

Ingredients

1	15-ounce container of ricotta cheese
$1/3$	cup of sugar
$1/4$	teaspoon of ground cardamom
1	pint of pistachio ice cream (I like the natural, non-colored variety here)
3	tablespoons of milk

Steps

1   Preheat the oven to 375°F. In a medium bowl, mix together the ricotta cheese, sugar, and cardamom. Spread the mixture out into a $1/2$ - inch layer in an ungreased cake pan (square or round is fine). Bake for 40-45 minutes or until the ricotta is firm to the touch. (The edges will brown, don't worry.) While baking, move to step 2.

2   Empty the pint of ice cream into your serving dish and allow the ice cream to melt while the ricotta is baking. Once melted, stir in the milk.

3   Once the ricotta cheese is out of the oven, wait until it is cool enough to handle. Cut the baked ricotta into squares or, for a more authentic look, use a cookie cutter to cut out discs. The cheese may be a bit crumbly, but the little cakes should generally hold together. (If not, bake for another 5 minutes.) Carefully transfer the individual pieces into the melted ice cream sauce. Refrigerate until serving. If desired, garnish with cardamom, nuts, or orange zest.

Serves several.

Tip: For a non-ice cream milk sauce, combine $1/2$ cup of sweetened condensed milk + 12 ounces of evaporated milk + $1/4$ cup of sugar + $1/4$ teaspoon of almond extract. Heat through and use this as your rasmalai milk sauce.

Puddings, Porridges, and Generations of Love

"I miss Bobo." "I miss her too," responds my four-year-old boy. We carry our laundry upstairs, walking by my mom's basement apartment, still dark almost a year later. On my way up, I pretend to drop a sock from my overflowing basket and my son leaps into action to save it from peril—one of his laundry duties and my many tricks to keep him an interested helper. As Mark climbs onto his seat at the kitchen counter, I ask him what he misses about my mom (who Mark nicknamed "Bobo").

I am curious how much he can remember about the grandmother who started living with us when he wasn't yet two, and who was gone before he turned four. She was diagnosed with terminal cancer when he was learning to speak in sentences. I remember her laughing with us when he exclaimed that he wanted "a BIG pee of cake!" All while her eyes carried a constant pool of water.

Remembering my mother, Mark smiles widely and I brace myself for one of those profound reflections that only a child can unwittingly render. He whispers, "when I came home from school, she would always give me a bar. And we didn't even tell you, mommy. We kept it a secret!" I know he's referring to the fruit and cereal bars that I usually didn't give him myself. "They were *so* yummy, mommy. I miss Bobo." At once, I felt a little let down that he remembered her for something so seemingly insignificant. (I was also relieved that I hadn't been too strict about their not-so-secret food exchanges.)

I guess when you're three years old, a pink-foiled raspberry cereal bar delivered with a warm hug and a covert smile really is everything in the world. And why not? It's sustenance and personal validation all in one. Some might call that love.

It now makes sense to me why grandparents of all generations and cultures attempt to spoil their grandchildren one way or another. Our first memories of our loving elders are often on simple and pure terms. Frankly, I don't know what I was expecting my son to say. "I really miss the way that Bobo would explain how her paintings were inspired by the brush strokes of Cassatt and Degas?" Or, "I miss the way she encouraged me to follow my dreams with a fire in my belly?" Those might be my answers today. But at age four, like Mark, I probably would have just said that I missed her quick breakfast porridge.

My mom would make creamy rice puddings, carrot halwa, and sweet Indian porridge (a simple Indian snack made of ground semolina). She always cooked the porridge on the stove with milk, not water. And she added a good helping of sugar or honey—she knew she was competing with the generic coco krispies in the cupboard. She even took the time to roast up nuts and raisins in butter in a separate pan, until the raisins plumped up into glistening spheres, and then she'd quickly spoon the golden nuts and raisins onto the steaming cereal.

In the pages that follow, I've shared my version of some of these puddings and porridges, which I still love today for dessert and breakfast.

At Mark's age, there's no way I would have been able to articulate that I was grateful for my mom getting up on a cold morning to make me breakfast while I snuggled in bed, or that I was thankful for how she'd always remember to pour a little cold milk on my porridge so that I could dig in right away without burning my tongue . . . or all those other things, big and small, that a parent or loved one does to protect and care for you. But as my mom always watched expectantly as I took my first bite, I think she knew what it meant when I looked up and simply said with a big grin, "yummy!" And so, I think I know what Mark means now . . . and I miss her too.

Coconut Rice Pudding _in 20 minutes_

This dessert is perfectly luscious and creamy. Traditional rice porridge cooks for a long time, so this is one recipe where using an instant rice actually makes sense. But you can easily make this pudding with leftover rice or fresh rice if you're up for it!

Ingredients

$3/4$ cup of minute rice (instant precooked parboiled rice) or 1 $1/3$ cup of leftover cooked white rice

$1^1/_2$ cups of coconut milk

$1^1/_2$ cups of milk

$1/4$ cup of sugar

1   teaspoon of vanilla

$1/4$ cup of raisins

$1/4$ cup of sweetened shredded coconut

$1/4$ cup of white chocolate chips or a small bar for shavings (optional)

Steps

1   In a medium pot over medium heat, thoroughly combine all the ingredients except the chocolate. Partially cover and cook for 10 minutes, stirring occasionally. Then reduce the heat to very low and fully cover, continuing to stir intermittently until the pudding is thick and creamy. (If the pudding starts to dry out, stir in extra milk or water, a tablespoon at a time.)

2   Once the pudding reaches the desired creamy texture (about 20 minutes or less) and your rice is fully cooked, remove from heat. As a final touch, you can top the pudding with white chocolate chips or chocolate shavings immediately before serving. (I just run a vegetable peeler over a bar of white chocolate and shave it directly over my bowl.)

Serves 4.

Tip: If you only have uncooked white rice, you can use $1/2$ cup and then you'll need to cook the pudding for about 15 minutes more.

Carrot Halwa Pudding *in 30 minutes*

Warm, delicate, and fudge-like—this pudding has all the flavors you love in carrot cake, without all the fuss.

Ingredients

4-5	carrots (you'll need about 2 cups worth)
2	tablespoons of butter
2	tablespoons of sugar
$1/2$	cup of milk
$1/2$	cup of sweetened condensed milk
$1/4$	cup of raisins
$1/4$	cup of chopped nuts (walnuts or pecans work well)
$1/4$	teaspoon of salt

Steps

1   Grate the carrots until you have about 2 cups worth. (This will take a few minutes, but the rest is simple. No matter what, don't use pre-grated carrots here; they will not lend the desired melt-in-your mouth texture.)

2   Melt the butter in a medium pot over medium heat and then add the carrots, sugar, and $1/4$ cup of the milk. Cover and stir occasionally, cooking the carrots for 10-12 minutes. (Add the remainder of the milk by the spoonful, if needed to keep the carrots moist.)

3   Stir the remaining ingredients into the pot. Cover and cook for about 10 more minutes, stirring occasionally. Add additional milk by the spoonful if the mixture ever becomes too dry. The finished carrot halwa should be moist and scoopable.

Serves 2-4.

Serve warm and top with whipped cream or ice cream, if desired.

Kesari *in 20 minutes*

Unlike many other Indian desserts, Kesari is not very sweet, and its subtle flavors and colors make it a great little dish to enjoy for breakfast, after a big meal, or with a nice cup of coffee or tea.

Ingredients

$1/8$	teaspoon saffron threads (a big pinch)
3	tablespoons of butter
$1/3$	cup of nuts (cashews or almonds)
$1/4$	cup of sugar
1	cup of milk
$1/8$	teaspoon of ground cardamom
$1/2$	cup of wheat farina cereal (cream of wheat)

Steps

1   Finely crush the saffron strands and set them aside. (You can use a mortar and pestle here if you have one, or just use the back of a big knife to grind down the strands against a cutting board.)

2   In a medium pot over medium heat, melt the butter. Meanwhile, roughly chop the nuts and then add them to the butter. Roast for 2-3 minutes. Add the sugar, milk, cardamom, saffron, and stir. Cover for a few minutes until the milk begins to bubble. Then, slowly stir in the cream of wheat and cook uncovered until all the liquid is absorbed and the cream of wheat has a mashed potato-like texture (should be done in 3-5 minutes). Remove from heat and serve.

Serves 2-4.

Serve warm or cold. For a pretty presentation, press the kesari into a small cup while still warm and then carefully invert the cup onto your serving plate to make a little tower of goodness.

Sweet Pongal *in 25 minutes*

Ingredients

- $\frac{1}{3}$ cup of red lentils (masoor dal)
- $\frac{2}{3}$ cup of white rice (preferably not long grain)
- 3   tablespoons of butter
- $\frac{1}{4}$ cup of raisins
- $\frac{1}{2}$ cup of nuts (I like to use almonds, pecans, or cashews)
- $\frac{1}{4}$ cup of honey
- $\frac{1}{4}$ cup of brown sugar
- 1   teaspoon of ground cardamom or cinnamon
- 1   teaspoon of vanilla (optional)

Steps

1   Combine the lentils and rice with $2\frac{2}{3}$ cup of water in a medium pot, partially covered, and cook for 15-20 minutes or until both the rice and lentils are fully cooked. (Or you can microwave them for 15-17 minutes.) Meanwhile, move to step 2.

2   Coarsely chop the nuts. Add 3 tablespoons of butter to a small pan over medium heat. Once the butter melts and is foaming, add in the raisins and nuts and roast them until the raisins plump up into spheres. Remove from heat and set aside.

3   Once the lentils and rice are fully cooked, stir in the roasted nuts and raisins along with the honey, brown sugar, and cardamom (and vanilla, if using), and cook together for 2-3 more minutes over medium heat.

Serves 2-4.

Serve hot and drizzle on extra honey, if desired.

Easy Indian Porridge *in 15 minutes*

Ingredients

$1/3$	cup of wheat farina cereal (cream of wheat)
2	cups of milk
$1/2$	teaspoon of vanilla extract
$1/8$	teaspoon of salt (a pinch)
$2^1/4$	tablespoons of sugar
2	tablespoons of butter
$1/4$	cup of raisins
$1/4$	cup of nuts (I like cashews or almonds)

Steps

1   Stir together the cream of wheat, milk, vanilla extract, salt, and sugar in a large glass dish and microwave for 5-6 minutes. (After about 2 minutes of microwaving, stop and give the porridge a good stir every minute or so.) Meanwhile, move to step 2.

2   Add the butter to a small pan over low-medium heat and allow it to melt and lightly foam. Once the butter turns golden brown, skim off the foam with a spoon and discard, leaving the browned melted or clarified butter in the pan. Stir in the raisins and nuts and cook them just until raisins plump up into spheres.

3   Pour the butter, nuts, and raisins over the porridge and serve hot.

Serves 2-4.

Sprinkle on cardamom or cinnamon, if desired.

Fruit Lassi *in 5 minutes*

This is a great smoothie that can be served anytime. Using mango juice or frozen fruit means I can always have the ingredients on hand. Feel free to substitute different fruits, but plain yogurt is the key to a more authentic lassi.

Ingredients

1   cup of plain yogurt
1   cup of mango juice or 1 cup of fresh or frozen whole strawberries
1   tablespoon of sugar (optional—I only add it if my fruit is not very ripe)

Steps

1   Prepare your fruit: if you are using fresh strawberries, remove the stems. If you are using frozen fruit, thaw it in the microwave for about 1 minute to soften.

2   Add all the ingredients into a blender and blend for 30 seconds to 1 minute. (At this point, the lassi should be ready to drink, but if it remains too thick, add a few tablespoons of water or milk and blend for 30 more seconds.)

Serves 2.

Serve immediately, plain or over ice.

Sweet Cardamom Nut Milk *in 5 minutes*

This rich drink is a great alternative to chai or hot cocoa. And for kids who want to play grown-up, it makes for a great kid-friendly "coffee."

Ingredients

2	tablespoons of creamy cashew nut or almond butter
$1^1/_2$	cups of milk
$^1/_4$	cup of sweetened condensed milk
$^1/_4$	teaspoon of ground cardamom

Steps

Add all the ingredients to a blender and blend for 30 seconds to 1 minute or until thoroughly mixed.

Serves 2.

If you want this cold, pour it over ice. Otherwise, warm a cupful in the microwave or on the stove.

Closing Time: The Emergency Cocktail

On occasion, it's nice to have a cocktail at your place with friends. Okay, maybe it's just you, but either way, having a couple of quick drinks at the ready is always a good idea.

Whatever your story, when closing time becomes an invitation to have the gang back to your place, you need to keep it simple. One of my go-to secret ingredients is ice cream. It already has the makings of a great drink—cold, creamy, and flavorful.

Here are two quick Indian-inspired drinks that will feed your spirit and cool your palate after the spiciest of meals. These are fairly basic, so feel free to improvise and add other flavors and liquors as the mood strikes. You also can't go wrong with a glass of wine, beer, or a mango spritzer (just equal parts mango juice and seltzer) with Indian food.

Coconut Rummers *in 5 minutes*

Ingredients

1	cup of coconut ice cream, gelato, or sorbet
2	ounces ($^1/_4$ cup) of rum
$^1/_2$	cup of water
$^1/_2$	cup of ice

Steps

Combine the ingredients in a blender and blend for 1 minute or until you've reached a smooth consistency. (You can also use a cocktail shaker, but then you'll want the ice cream to be softened first and may want to use crushed ice.)

Serves 2.

Mango Creamsicle *in 5 minutes*

Ingredients

1	cup of mango ice cream (or mango sorbet for a tangier version)
2	ounces ($^1/_4$ cup) of vodka
$^1/_2$	cup of water
$^1/_2$	cup of ice

Steps

Follow the same steps for blending the Coconut Rummers in the recipe above and enjoy!

Serves 2.

About the Author

The daughter of Indian immigrants, Varu Chilakamarri learned about the authentic, labor-intensive cooking style of Indian cuisine from her parents. Over the last twenty years, she has been adapting many traditional Indian dishes and creating shortcuts to fit her own busy lifestyle.

Varu is an attorney in Washington, D.C. From working on complex cases to a stint at the White House, she can relate to the stress of having a hectic life and not having a lot of time to cook. She has no formal culinary training—she's just discovered some tricks to being a vegetarian who endeavors to juggle a complicated cuisine with a full-time career, family, and friends. She's published several food essays and contributed to the Huffington Post. Varu lives in Capitol Hill with her husband Michael, their son Mark, and Lucy the cat.

Acknowledgments

There would be no book without my mom, Vachu Chilakamarri, and my dad, Kiran Chilakamarri. My parents taught me about Indian food, life, and determination, and I like to think this book reflects a little bit of all three.

To my husband, for his tireless and true support of all my endeavors, and to our son, for giving me a reason to put this out into the world. To our family, for always being in our corner. And to the dear friends and colleagues over the years who encouraged and inspired me to cook and share my ideas—from the amazing judicial clerks who hosted my first recipe-testing party, to my bosom friends who are always willing to taste something new.

Index

Page numbers in *italics* refer to illustrations.

CPSIA information can be obtained
at www.ICGtesting.com
Printed in the USA
LVHW070121050121
675573LV00004B/199

9 780578 651880